Dinah Zike's
Reading and Study Skills

FOLDABLES™

**Glencoe
McGraw-Hill**

New York, New York   Columbus, Ohio   Chicago, Illinois   Peoria, Illinois   Woodland Hills, California

Glencoe/McGraw-Hill

A Division of The McGraw·Hill Companies

Send all inquiries to:
Glencoe/McGraw-Hill
8787 Orion Place
Columbus, OH 43240-4027

ISBN 0-07-829148-8

Printed in the United States of America

1 2 3 4 5 6 7 8 9 10 079 08 07 06 05 04 03 02

Table of Contents

Introduction to Foldables

Folding Instructions

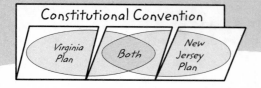

Chapter-Specific Foldables 49

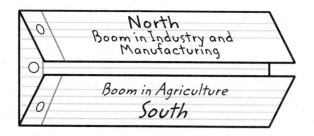

Dear Teacher,

What is a Foldable?

A Foldable is a 3-D, student-made, interactive graphic organizer based upon a skill. Making a Foldable gives students a fast, kinesthetic activity that helps them organize and retain information. Every chapter in the student edition of the textbook begins with a Foldable that is used as a Study Organizer. Each chapter's Foldable is designed to be used as a study guide for the main ideas and key points presented in sections of the chapter. Foldables can also be used for a more in-depth investigation of a concept, idea, opinion, event, or a person or place studied in a chapter. The purpose of this ancillary is to show you how to create various types of Foldables and provide chapter-specific Foldables examples. With this information, you can individualize Foldables to meet your curriculum needs.

This book is divided into two sections. The first section presents step-by-step instructions, illustrations, and photographs of 34 Foldables, many of which were not used in the student edition. I've included over 100 photographs to help you visualize ways in which they might enhance instruction. The second section presents two extra ideas on how to use Foldables for each chapter in the textbook. You can use the instruction section to design your own Foldables or alter the Foldables presented in each chapter as well. I highly suggest making this book available as a source for students who wish to learn new and creative ways in which to make study guides, present projects, or do extra credit work.

Who Am I?

You may have seen Foldables featured in this book used in supplemental programs or staff-development workshops. Today my Foldables are used internationally. I present workshops and keynotes to over fifty thousand teachers and parents a year, sharing Foldables that I began inventing, designing, and adapting over thirty five years ago. Students of all ages are using them for daily work, note-taking activities, student-directed projects, forms of alternative assessment, journals, graphs, tables, and more.

Have fun using and adapting Foldables,

Why use Foldables in Social Studies?

When teachers ask me why they should take time to use the Foldables featured in this book, I explain that they:

. . . organize, display, and arrange information, making it easier for students to grasp social studies concepts, theories, facts, opinions, questions, research, and ideas.

. . . are student-made study guides that are compiled as students listen for main ideas, read for main ideas, or conduct research.

. . . provide a multitude of creative formats in which students can present projects, research, interviews, and inquiry-based reports.

. . . replace teacher-generated writing or photocopied sheets with student-generated print.

. . . incorporate the use of such skills as comparing and contrasting, recognizing cause and effect, and finding similarities and differences.

. . . continue to "immerse" students in previously learned vocabulary, concepts, information, generalizations, ideas, and theories, providing them with a strong foundation that they can build upon with new observations, concepts, and knowledge.

. . . can be used by students or teachers to easily communicate data through graphs, tables, charts, models, and diagrams, including Venn diagrams.

. . . allow students to make their own journals for recording observations, research information, primary and secondary source data, surveys, and so on.

. . . can be used as alternative assessment tools by teachers to evaluate student progress or by students to evaluate their own progress.

. . . integrate language arts, the sciences, and mathematics into the study of social studies.

. . . provide a sense of student ownership or investiture in the social studies curriculum.

Foldables and the NCSS Thematic Strands

In *Curriculum Standards for Social Studies: Expectations of Excellence,* the National Council for the Social Studies (NCSS) identified 10 themes that serve as organizing strands for the social studies curriculum at every school level. The themes include:

I.   Culture
II.   Time, Continuity, and Change
III.   People, Places, and Environments
IV.   Individual Development and Identity
V.   Individuals, Groups, and Institutions
VI.   Power, Authority, and Governance
VII.   Production, Distribution, and Consumption
VIII. Science, Technology, and Society
IX.   Global Connections
X.   Civic Ideals and Practices

Students are expected to master specific skills that are organized around these themes, such as analyzing data, comparing and contrasting similarities and differences, explaining and describing concepts, and identifying cause-and-effect relationships.

Foldables help students practice and master these specific skills. Foldables require students to identify and describe main ideas, relationships, and processes. In most cases, students need to understand and comprehend information before they can illustrate it in a foldable. Foldables help students think, analyze, and communicate.

Foldable Basics

What to Write and Where

Teach students to write general information such as titles, vocabulary words, concepts, questions, main ideas, and dates on the front tabs of their Foldables. This way students can easily recognize main ideas and important concepts. Foldables help students focus on and remember key points without being distracted by other print.

Ask students to write specific information such as supporting ideas, student thoughts, answers to questions, research information, class notes, observations, and definitions under the tabs.

As you teach, demonstrate different ways in which Foldables can be used. Soon you will find that students make their own Foldables and use them independently for study guides and projects.

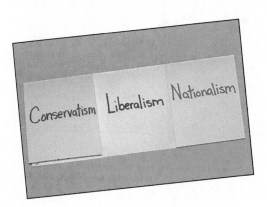
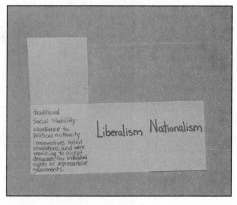

With or Without Tabs

Foldables with flaps or tabs create study guides that students can use to check what they know about the general information on the front of tabs. Use Foldables without tabs for assessment purposes or projects where information is presented for others to view quickly.

Venn diagram used as a study guide

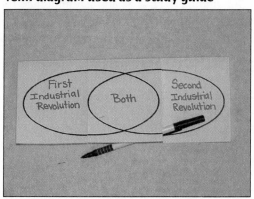

Venn diagram used for assessment

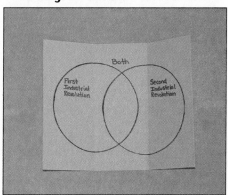

What to Do With Scissors and Glue

If it is difficult for your students to keep glue and scissors at their desks, set up a small table in the classroom and provide several containers of glue, numerous pairs of scissors (sometimes tied to the table), containers of crayons and colored pencils, a stapler, clear tape, and anything else you think students might need to make their Foldables.

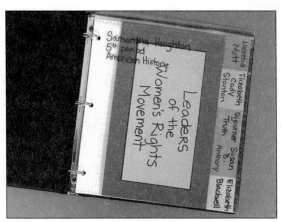

Storing Foldables

There are several ways that students can store their Foldables. They can use grocery bags, plastic bags, or shoeboxes. Students can also punch holes in their Foldables and place them in a three-ring binder. Suggest they place strips of two-inch clear tape along one side and punch three holes through the taped edge.

By keeping all of their Foldables together and organized, students will have created their own portfolio.

HINT: *I found it more convenient to keep student portfolios in my classroom so student work was always available when needed. Giant detergent boxes make good storage containers for portfolios.*

Use This Book as a Creative Resource

Have this book readily available for students to use as an idea reference for projects, discussions, social studies debates, extra credit work, cooperative learning group presentations, and so on. Encourage students to think of their own versions of Foldables to help them learn the material the best way possible.

Using Visuals and Graphics With Foldables

The graphics on pages 6–12 can be used as visual aids for students' Foldables. Students can incorporate them into their journals, notes, projects, and study guides independently. I found that students and teachers were more likely to use graphics if they were available on a classroom computer where they could be selected and printed out as needed. You can also photocopy and distribute the pages that follow for students to trace or cut out for their projects. All these visuals will aid student understanding and retention.

1. Students can mark and label large United States and world maps to show where past and recent events occurred, where a historic person lived and worked, where wars were fought and battles won, where volcanoes are active and inactive, where boundaries of territories or regions existed, and so on.

2. Students can mark and label smaller maps of continents to illustrate more specific locations. For example, when making a *who, what, when, where* Foldable, students can identify exactly where the particular event occurred or where the individual lived.

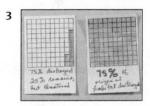

3. Bar graphs, grids, and circle graphs can be used to show changes over time, population distribution, and so on.

4. Use time lines to record when someone lived or when an event or sequence of events occurred. Use two time lines to compare what was happening in two different areas at the same time.

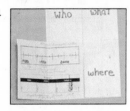

5. Use small picture frames to sketch or name a person, place, or thing.

Africa

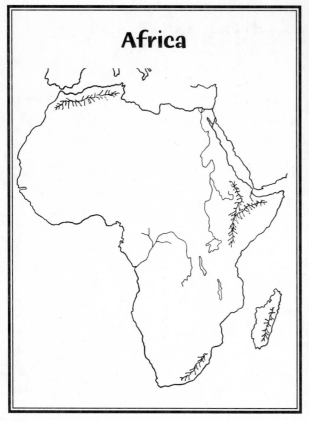

Antarctica

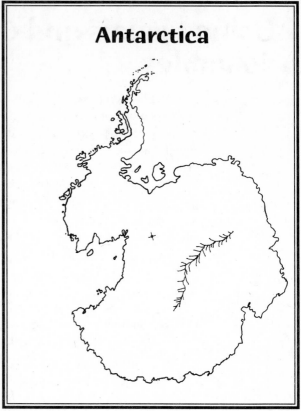

Asia

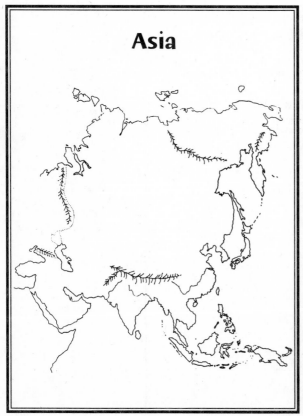

Australia

Europe

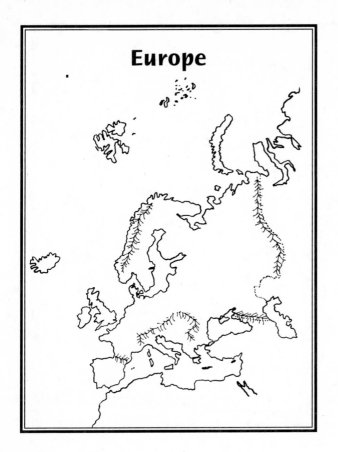

North America

South America

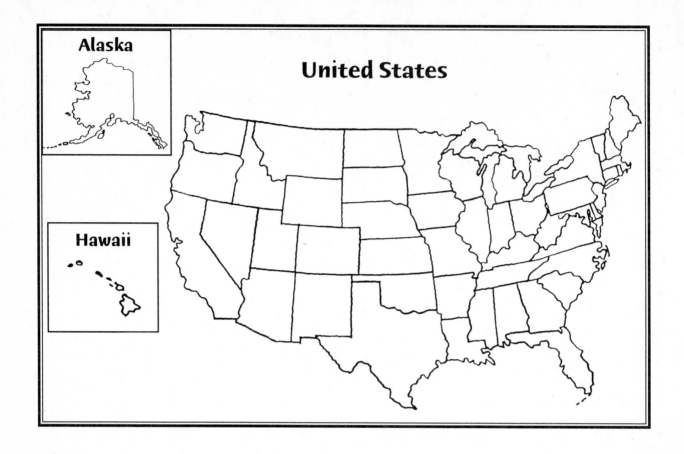

Alaska

Hawaii

United States

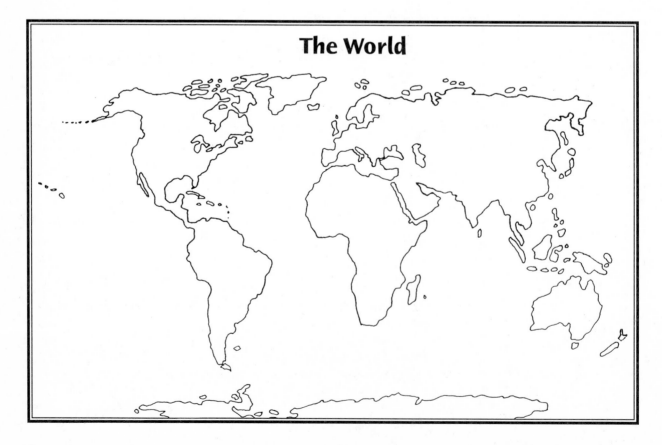

The World

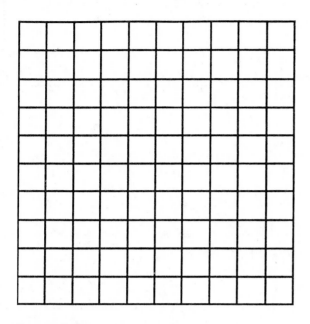

Percentages or bar graph

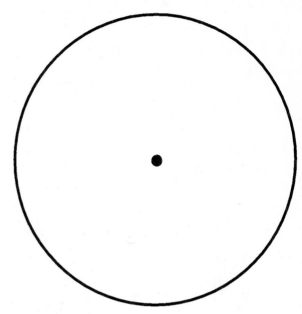

Circle graph

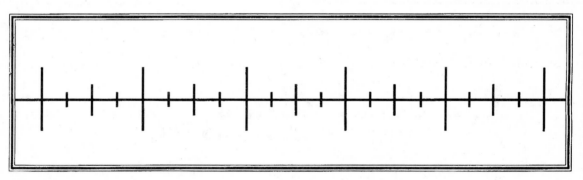

Generic Time Line

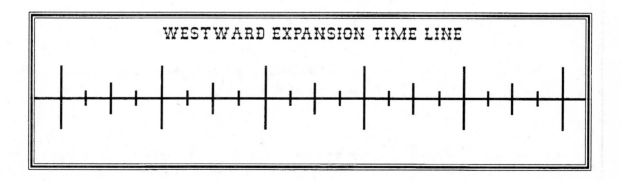

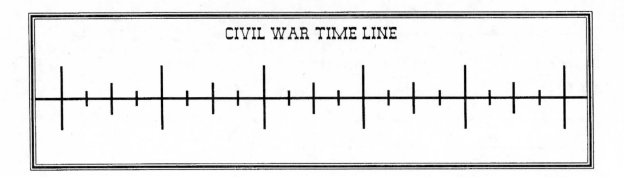

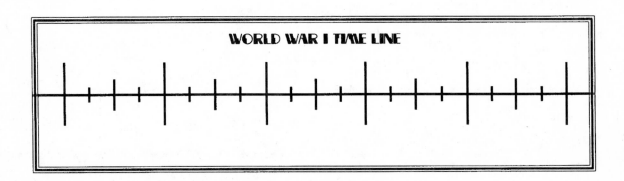

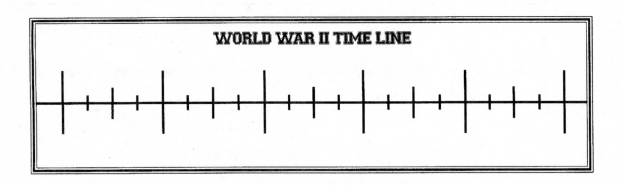

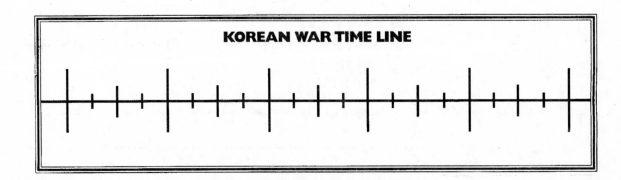

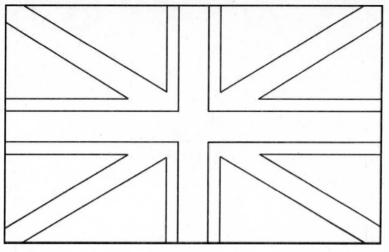

England

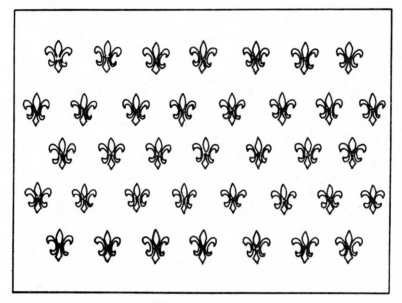

France

Spain

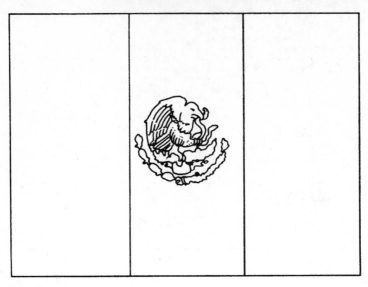

Mexico

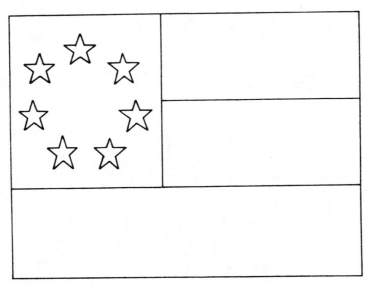

Confederacy

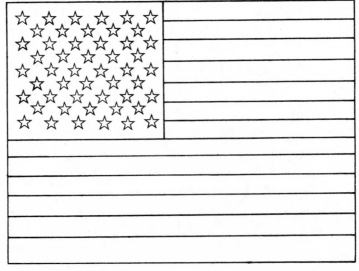

United States of America

Basic Foldables Shapes

The following figures illustrate the basic folds that are referred to throughout the instruction section of this book.

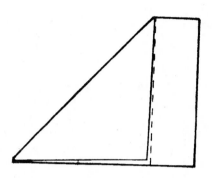

Taco Fold

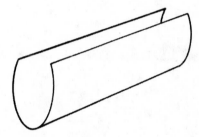

Hamburger Fold

Hot Dog Fold

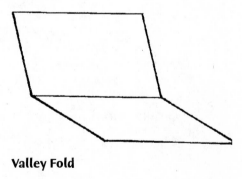

Burrito Fold

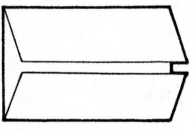

Shutter Fold

Valley Fold

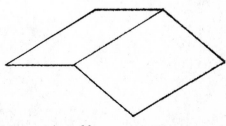

Mountain Fold

Half Book

Fold a sheet of paper in half.

1. This book can be folded vertically like a *hot dog* or . . .

2. . . . it can be folded horizontally like a *hamburger.*

Use this book for descriptive, expository, persuasive, or narrative writing, as well as graphs, diagrams, or charts.

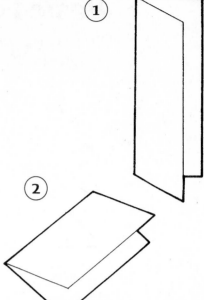

Folded Book

1. Make a *half-book*. (p. 14)

2. Fold it in half again like a *hamburger*. This makes a ready-made cover and two small pages for information on the inside.

Use photocopied work sheets, Internet printouts, and student-drawn diagrams or maps to make this book. One sheet of paper becomes two activities and two grades.

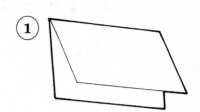

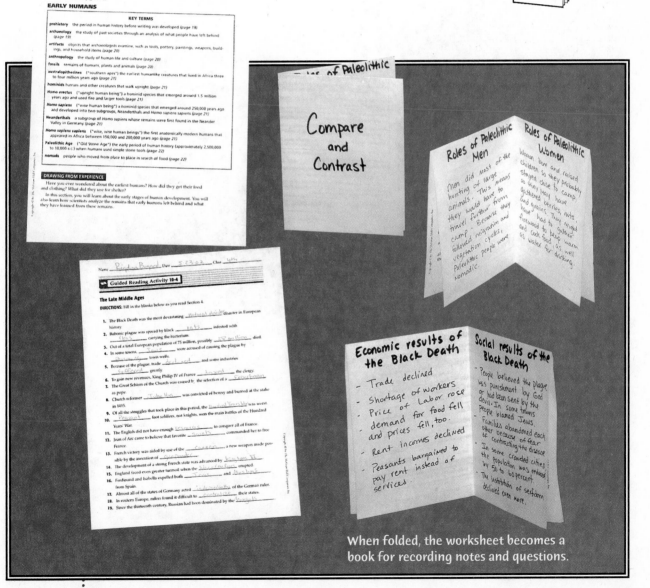

When folded, the worksheet becomes a book for recording notes and questions.

Three-Quarter Book

1. Make a *two-tab book* (p. 18) and raise the left-hand tab.

2. Cut the tab off at the top fold line.

3. A larger book of information can be made by gluing several *three-quarter books* side by side.

Sketch or glue a graphic to the left, write one or more questions on the right, and record answers and information under the right tab.

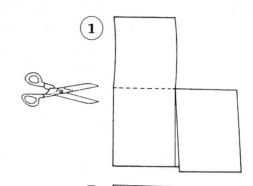

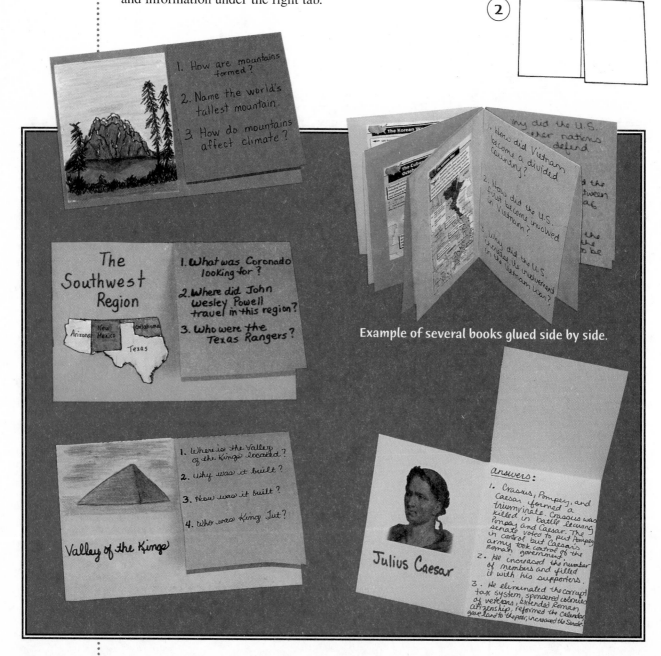

Example of several books glued side by side.

Bound Book

1. Take two sheets of paper and fold them separately like a *hamburger*. Place the papers on top of each other, leaving one-sixteenth of an inch between the *mountain tops*.

2. Mark both folds one inch from the outer edges.

3. On one of the folded sheets, cut slits in the middle to the marked spot on both sides.

4. On the second folded sheet, start at one of the marked spots and cut the fold between the two marks.

5. Take the cut sheet from step 3 and fold it like a *burrito*. Place the *burrito* through the other sheet and then open the *burrito*. Fold the bound pages in half to form an eight-page book.

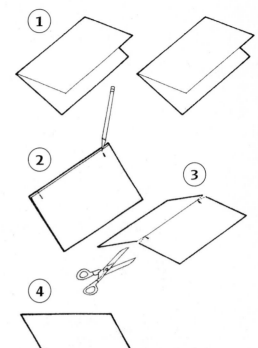

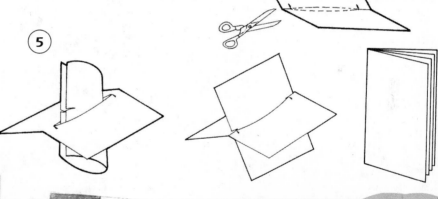

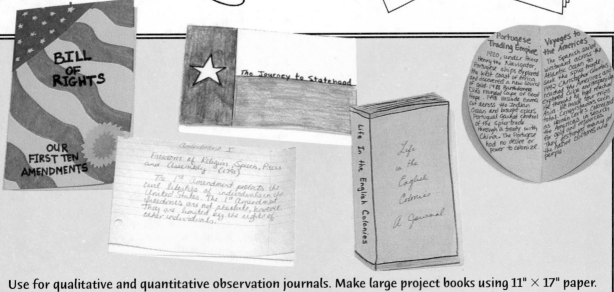

Use for qualitative and quantitative observation journals. Make large project books using 11" × 17" paper.

Two-Tab Book

1. Make a *folded book* (p. 15) and cut up the *valley* of the inside fold toward the *mountain top*. This cut forms two large tabs that can be used for text and illustrations on the front and back.

2. The book can be expanded by making several of these folds and gluing them side by side.

Use this book for learning about two things. For example, use it for comparing and contrasting, determining cause and effect, finding similarities and differences, using Venn diagrams, and so on.

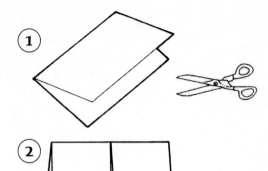

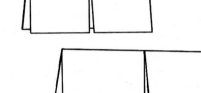

Pocket Book

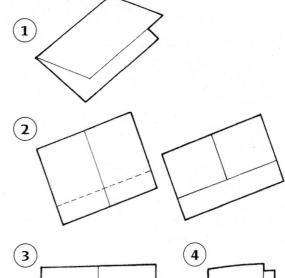

1. Fold a sheet of paper in half like a *hamburger.*

2. Open the folded paper and fold one of the long sides up two inches to form a pocket. Refold along the *hamburger* fold so that the newly formed pockets are on the inside.

3. Glue the outer edges of the two-inch fold with a small amount of glue.

4. **Optional:** Glue a cover around the *pocket book.*

   Variation: Make a multi-paged booklet by gluing several pockets side by side. Glue a cover around the multi-paged *pocket book.*

Summarize information on note cards or on quarter sheets of notebook paper. Store other foldables, such as *two-tab books,* inside the pockets.

Matchbook

1. Fold a sheet of paper like a *hamburger,* but fold it so that one side is one inch longer than the other side.

2. Fold the one-inch tab over the short side forming a fold like an envelope.

3. Cut the front flap in half toward the *mountain top* to create two flaps.

Use this book to report on one thing, such as a person, place, or thing, or for reporting on two things, such as the cause and effect of Western Expansion.

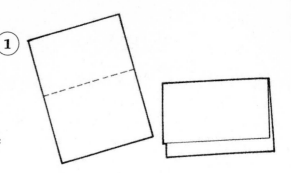

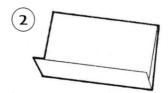

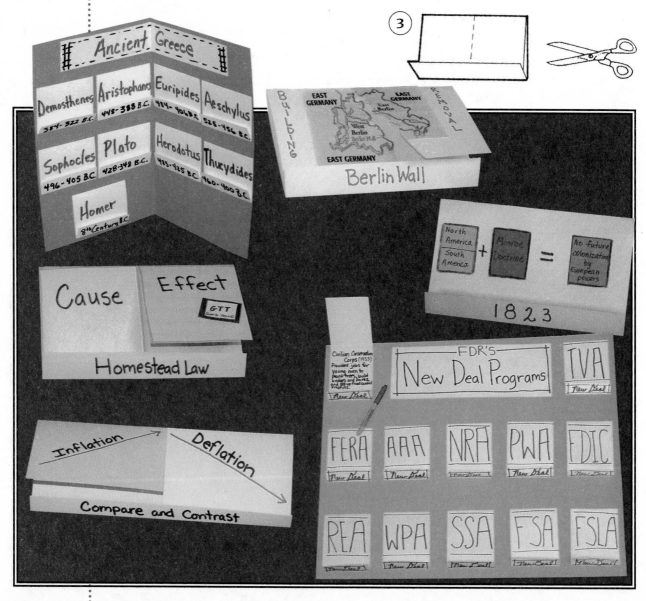

Shutter Fold

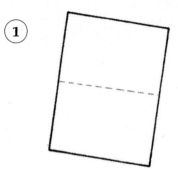

1. Begin as if you were going to make a *hamburger* but instead of creasing the paper, pinch it to show the midpoint.

2. Fold the outer edges of the paper to meet at the pinch, or mid-point, forming a *shutter fold*.

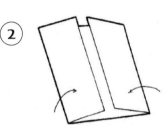

Use this book for comparing two things. Students could also make this foldable with 11" × 17" paper and then glue smaller books—such as the *half book, journal,* and *two-tab book*—inside to create a large project full of student work.

Trifold Book

1. Fold a sheet of paper into thirds.

2. Use this book as is, or cut into shapes. If the trifold is cut, leave plenty of paper on both sides of the designed shape, so the book will open and close in three sections.

Use this book to make charts with three columns or rows, large Venn diagrams, reports on three events or people, or to show and explain the outside and inside of something.

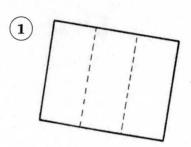

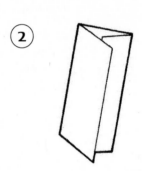

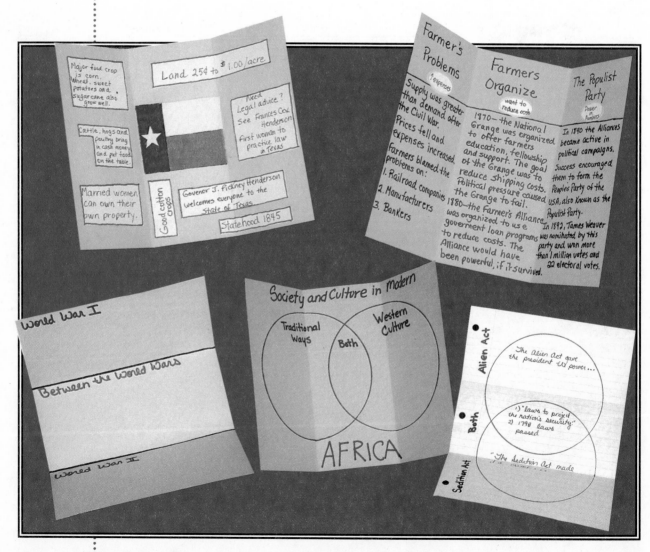

Three-Tab Book

1. Fold a sheet of paper like a *hot dog*.

2. With the paper horizontal, and the fold of the *hot dog* up, fold the right side toward the center, trying to cover one-third of the paper.

   NOTE: *If you fold the right edge over first, the final foldable will open and close like a book.*

3. Fold the left side over the right side to make a book with three folds.

4. Open the folded book. Place your hands between the two thicknesses of paper and cut up the two *valleys* on the top layer only along both folds. This will make three tabs.

Use this book for writing information about three things and for Venn diagrams.

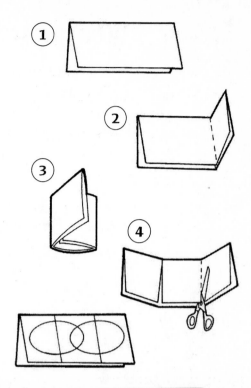

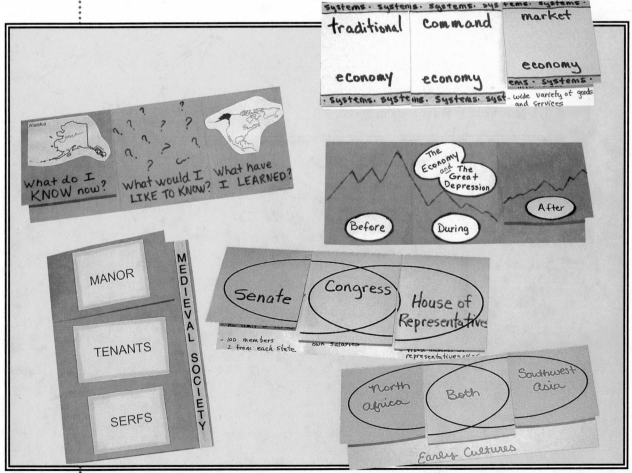

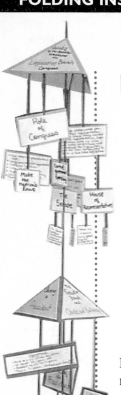

Pyramid Fold

1. Fold a sheet of paper into a *taco*, forming a square. Cut off the leftover piece.

2. Fold the triangle in half. Unfold. The folds will form an X dividing four equal sections.

3. Cut up one fold line and stop at the middle. Draw an X on one tab and label the other three.

4. Fold the X flap under the other flap and glue together. This makes a three-sided pyramid.

Label front sections and write information, notes, thoughts, and questions inside the pyramid on the back of the appropriate tab.

Use to make mobiles and dioramas.

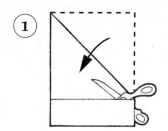

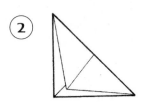

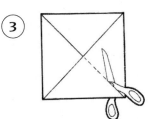

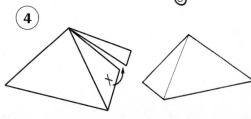

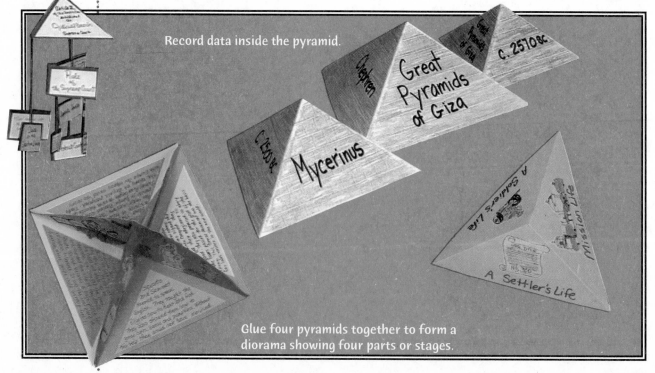

Record data inside the pyramid.

Glue four pyramids together to form a diorama showing four parts or stages.

Layered-Look Book

1. Stack two sheets of paper so that the back sheet is one inch higher than the front sheet.

2. Fold up the bottom edges of the paper to form four tabs. Align the edges so that all of the layers or tabs are the same distance apart.

3. When all tabs are the same size, crease the paper to hold the tabs in place and staple or glue the sheets together.

Glue the sheets together along the *valley* or inner center fold or staple them along the *mountain top*.

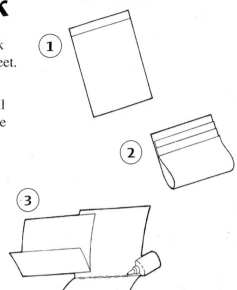

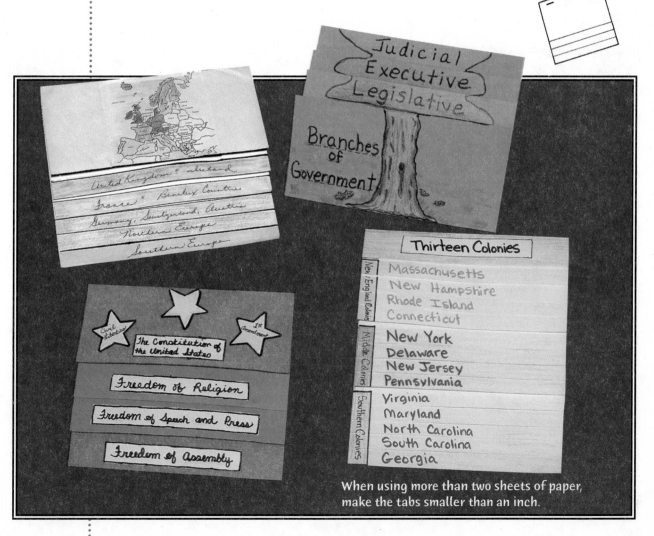

When using more than two sheets of paper, make the tabs smaller than an inch.

Four-Tab Book

1. Fold a sheet of paper in half like a *hot dog*.

2. Fold this long rectangle in half like a *hamburger*.

3. Fold both ends back to touch the *mountain top*.

4. On the side with two *valleys* and one *mountain top*, cut along the three inside fold lines on the front flap to make four tabs.

Use this book for recording information on four things, events, or people.

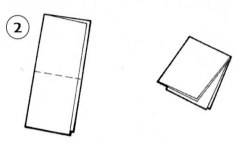

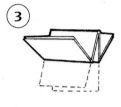

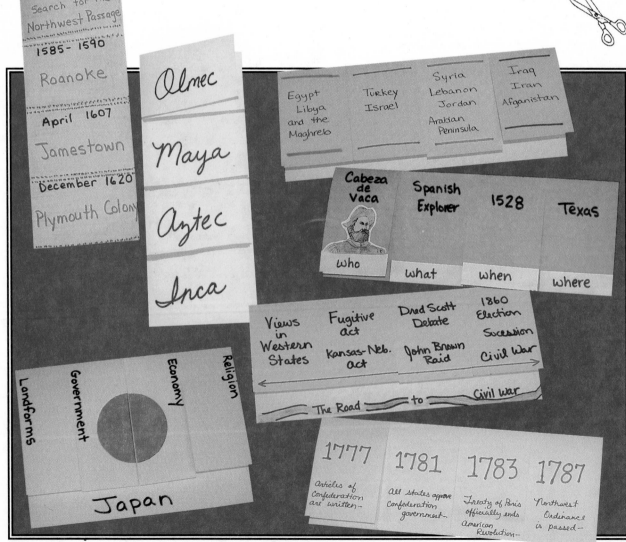

Standing Cube

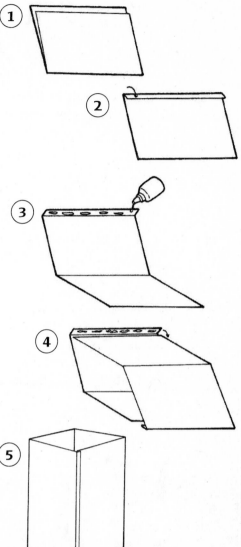

1. Use two sheets of the same size paper. Fold each like a *hamburger.* However, fold one side one-half inch shorter than the other side. This will make a tab that extends out one-half inch on one side.

2. Fold the long side over the short side of both sheets of paper, making tabs.

3. On one of the folded papers, place a small amount of glue along the the small folded tab next to the *valley,* but not in it.

4. Place the non-folded edge of the second sheet of paper square into the *valley* and fold the glue-covered tab over this sheet of paper. Press flat until the glue holds. Repeat with the other side.

5. Allow the glue to dry completely before continuing. After the glue has dried, the cube can be collapsed flat to allow students to work at their desks.

Use the cube for organizing information on four things. Use 11" × 17" paper to make larger project cubes that you can glue other foldables onto for display. Notebook paper, photocopied sheets, magazine pictures, and current events articles can also be displayed on the larger cubes.

These cubes can be stored in plastic bag portfolios by collapsing the cubes to make them flat.

Envelope Fold

1. Fold a sheet of paper into a *taco* forming a square. Cut off the leftover piece.

2. Open the folded *taco* and refold it the opposite way forming another *taco* and an X-fold pattern.

3. Open the *taco fold* and fold the corners toward the center point of the X forming a small square.

4. Trace this square onto another sheet of paper. Cut and glue it to the inside of the envelope. Pictures can be placed under or on top of the tabs.

Use this foldable for organizing information on four things. Use it for "hidden pictures" and current events pictures. Have your classmates raise one tab at a time until they can guess what the picture represents. Number the tabs in the order in which they are to be opened.

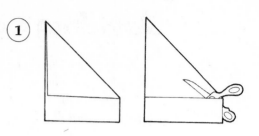

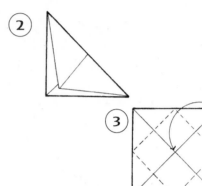

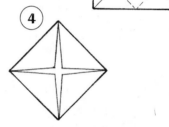

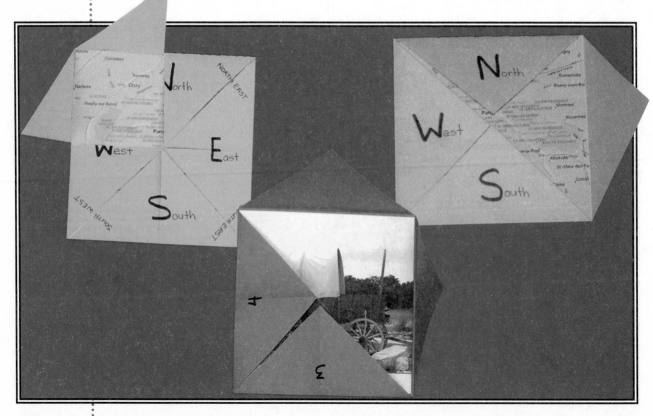

Four-Door Book

1. Make a *shutter fold* (p. 21) using a larger sheet of paper.

2. Fold the *shutter fold* in half like a *hamburger.* Crease well.

3. Open the project and cut along the two inside *valley* folds.

4. These cuts will form four doors on the inside of the project.

Use this book for organizing information on four things. When folded in half like a *hamburger,* a finished *four-door book* can be glued inside a large (11" × 17") *shutter fold* as part of a more inclusive project.

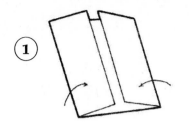
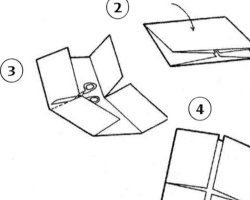
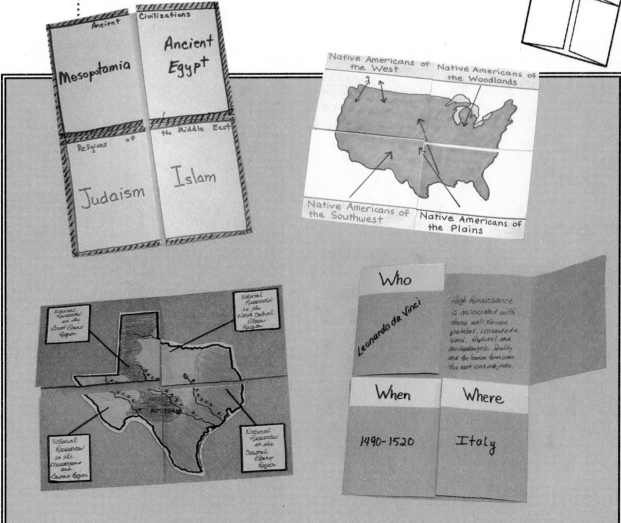

Top-Tab Book

1. Fold a sheet of paper in half like a *hamburger.* Cut the center fold, forming two half sheets.

2. Fold one of the half sheets four times. Begin by folding it in half like a *hamburger,* fold again like a *hamburger,* and finally again like a *hamburger.* This folding has formed your pattern of four rows and four columns, or 16 small squares.

3. Fold two sheets of paper in half like a *hamburger.* Cut the center folds, forming four half sheets.

4. Hold the pattern vertically and place on a half sheet of paper under the pattern. Cut the bottom right hand square out of both sheets. Set this first page aside.

5. Take a second half sheet of paper and place it under the pattern. Cut the first and second right hand squares out of both sheets. Place the second page on top of the first page.

(continued next page)

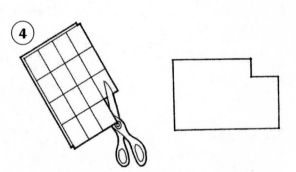

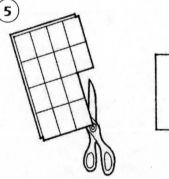

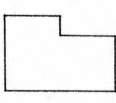

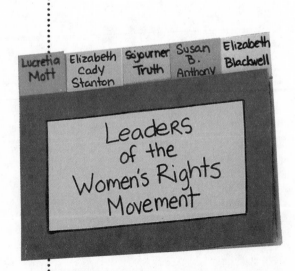

6. Take a third half sheet of paper and place it under the pattern. Cut the first, second, and third right hand squares out of both sheets. Place this third page on top of the second page.

7. Place the fourth, uncut half sheet of paper behind the three cut out sheets, leaving four aligned tabs across the top of the book. Staple several times on the left side. You can also place glue along the left paper edges and stack them together.

8. Cut a final half sheet of paper with no tabs and staple along the left side to form a cover.

Use this foldable to organize several events or characteristics of a person, place, or occurrence.

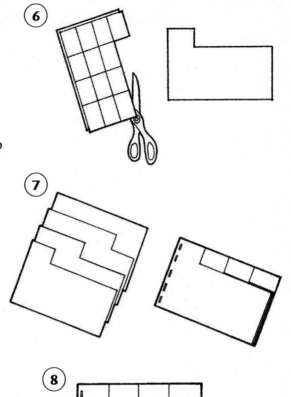

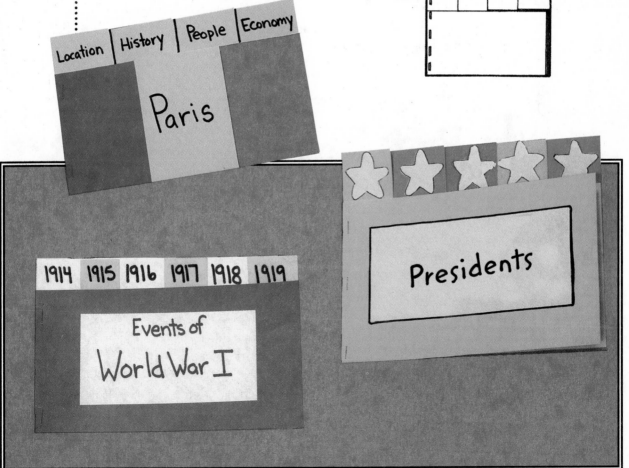

Accordion Book

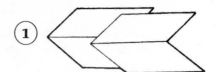

1. Fold two sheets of paper into *hamburgers*.

2. Cut the sheets of paper in half along the fold lines.

3. Fold each section of paper into *hamburgers*. However, fold one side one-half inch shorter than the other side. This will form a tab that is one-half inch long.

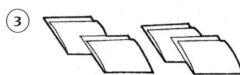

4. Fold this tab forward over the shorter side, and then fold it back from the shorter piece of paper. (In other words, fold it the opposite way.)

5. Glue together to form an *accordion* by gluing a straight edge of one section into the *valley* of another section.

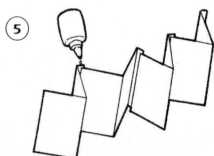

NOTE: *Stand the sections on end to form an* accordion *to help students visualize how to glue them together. See illustration.*

Always place the extra tab at the back of the book so you can add more pages later.

Use this book for time lines, sequencing events or information, biographies, and so on.

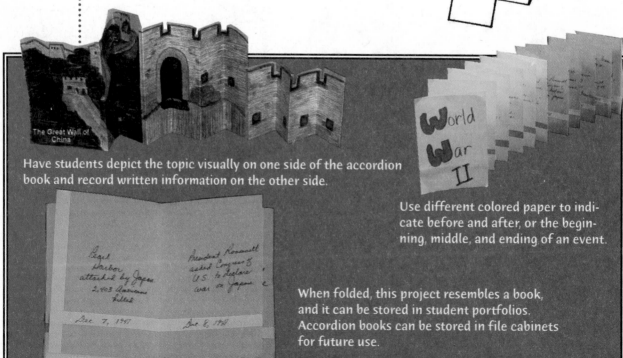

Have students depict the topic visually on one side of the accordion book and record written information on the other side.

Use different colored paper to indicate before and after, or the beginning, middle, and ending of an event.

When folded, this project resembles a book, and it can be stored in student portfolios. Accordion books can be stored in file cabinets for future use.

The Great Wall of China

World War II

Pearl Harbor attacked by Japan 2,403 Americans killed

President Roosevelt asked Congress to U.S. to declare war on Japan

Dec. 7, 1941

Dec. 8, 1941

Pop-Up Book

1. Fold a sheet of paper in half like a *hamburger*.

2. Beginning at the fold, or *mountain top,* cut one or more tabs.

3. Fold the tabs back and forth several times until there is a good fold line formed.

4. Partially open the *hamburger* fold and push the tabs through to the inside.

5. With one small dot of glue, glue figures for the *pop-up book* to the front of each tab. Allow the glue to dry before going on to the next step.

6. Make a cover for the book by folding another sheet of paper in half like a *hamburger.* Place glue around the outside edges of the *pop-up book* and firmly press inside the *hamburger* cover.

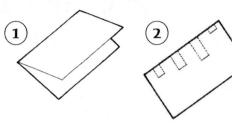

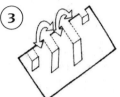

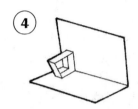

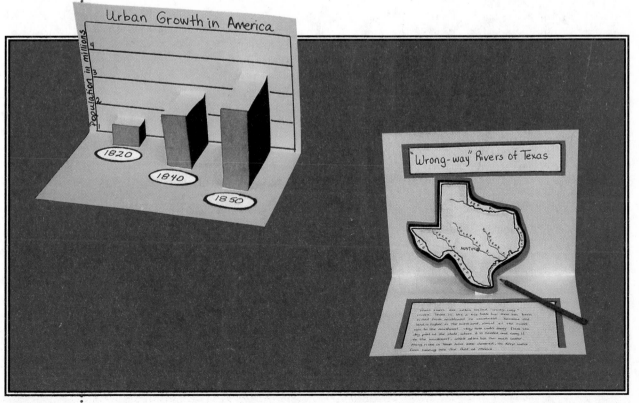

Five-Tab Book

1. Fold a sheet of paper in half like a *hot dog*.

2. Fold the paper so that one-third is exposed and two-thirds are covered.

3. Fold the two-thirds section in half.

4. Fold the one-third section (single thickness) backward to form a fold line.

The paper will be divided into fifths when opened. Use this foldable to organize information about five countries, dates, events, and so on.

①

② 1/3 | 2/3

③

④

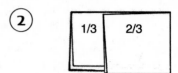

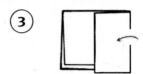

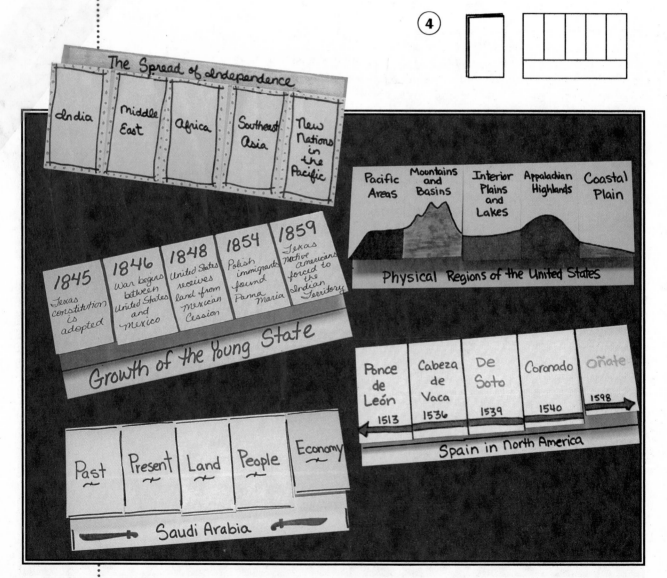

The Spread of Independence

India | Middle East | Africa | Southeast Asia | New Nations in the Pacific

1845 Texas constitution is adopted | 1846 War begins between United States and Mexico | 1848 United States receives land from Mexican Cession | 1854 Polish immigrants found Panna Maria | 1859 Texas native americans forced to the Indian Territory

Growth of the Young State

Pacific Areas | Mountains and Basins | Interior Plains and Lakes | Appaladian Highlands | Coastal Plain

Physical Regions of the United States

Ponce de León 1513 | Cabeza de Vaca 1536 | De Soto 1539 | Coronado 1540 | Oñate 1598

Spain in North America

Past | Present | Land | People | Economy

Saudi Arabia

Folded Table or Chart

1. Fold a sheet of paper into the number of vertical columns needed to make the table or chart.

2. Fold the horizontal rows needed to make the table or chart.

3. Label the rows and columns.

REMEMBER: Tables are organized along vertical and horizontal axes, while charts are organized along one axis, either horizontal or vertical.

Fold the sheet of paper into as many columns or rows that you need for the particular topic.

Table

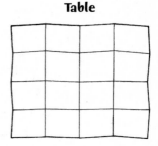

Chart

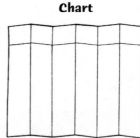

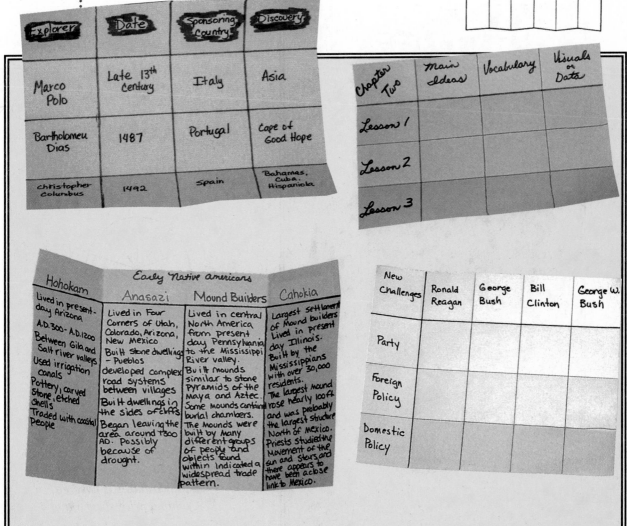

Explorer	Date	Sponsoring Country	Discovery
Marco Polo	Late 13th Century	Italy	Asia
Bartholomeu Dias	1487	Portugal	Cape of Good Hope
Christopher Columbus	1492	Spain	Bahamas, Cuba, Hispaniola

Chapter Two	Main Ideas	Vocabulary	Visuals or Data
Lesson 1			
Lesson 2			
Lesson 3			

Early Native americans

Hohokam	Anasazi	Mound Builders	Cahokia
Lived in present-day Arizona. A.D.300-A.D.1200 Between Gila and Salt river valleys. Used irrigation canals. Pottery, carved stone, etched shells. Traded with coastal people.	Lived in Four Corners of Utah, Colorado, Arizona, New Mexico. Built stone dwellings – Pueblos. developed complex road systems between villages. Built dwellings in the sides of cliffs. Began leaving the area around 1300 AD. Possibly because of drought.	Lived in central North America from present day Pennsylvania to the Mississippi River valley. Built mounds similar to stone Pyramids of the Maya and Aztec. Some mounds contained burial chambers. The Mounds were built by many different groups of people and objects found within Indicated a widespread trade pattern.	Largest settlement of Mound builders. Lived in present day Illinois. Built by the Mississippians with over 30,000 residents. The largest mound rose nearly 100ft and was probably the largest structure North of Mexico. Priests studied the Movement of the sun and stars and there appears to have been a close link to Mexico.

New Challenges	Ronald Reagan	George Bush	Bill Clinton	George W. Bush
Party				
Foreign Policy				
Domestic Policy				

Folding a Circle Into Tenths

1. Cut a circle out of a sheet of paper. Then fold the circle in half.

2. Fold the half circle so that one-third is exposed and two-thirds are covered.

3. Fold the one-third (single thickness) backward to form a fold line.

4. Fold the two-thirds section in half.

5. The half circle will be divided into fifths. When opened, the circle will be divided into tenths.

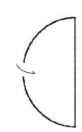 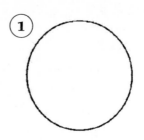

 2/3

1/3

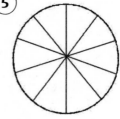

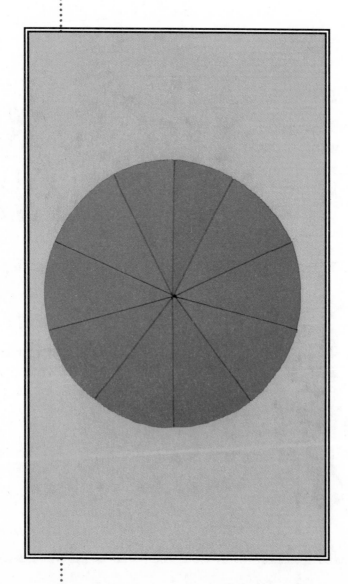

NOTE: *Paper squares and rectangles are folded into tenths the same way. Fold them so that one-third is exposed and two-thirds is covered. Continue with steps 3 and 4.*

Circle Graph

1. Cut out two circles from two sheets of paper.

2. Fold one of the circles in half on each axis, forming fourths. Cut along one of the fold lines (the radius) to the middle of each circle. Flatten the circle.

3. Place the two circles together along the cuts until they overlap completely.

4. Spin one of the circles while holding the other still. Estimate how much of each of the two (or you can add more) circles should be exposed to illustrate percentages or categories of information. Add circles to represent more than two percentages.

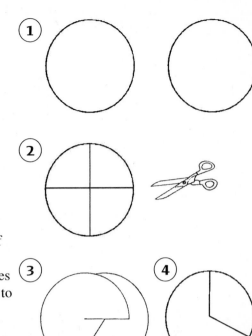

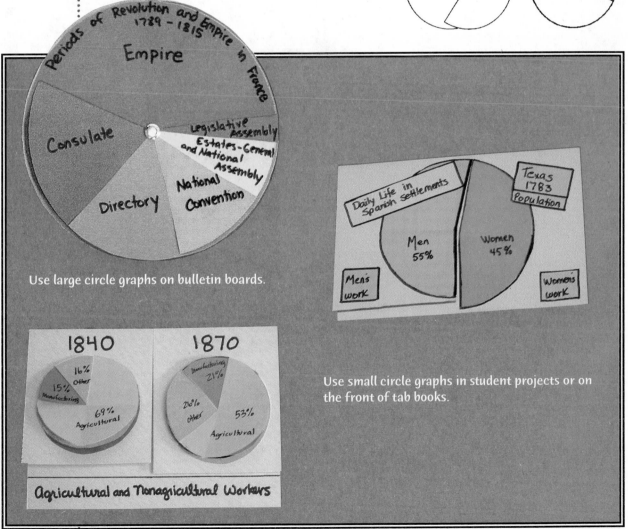

Use large circle graphs on bulletin boards.

Use small circle graphs in student projects or on the front of tab books.

Concept-Map Book

1. Fold a sheet of paper along the long or short axis, leaving a two-inch tab uncovered along the top.

2. Fold in half or in thirds.

3. Unfold and cut along the two or three inside fold lines.

Use this book to write facts about a person, place, or thing under the appropriate tab.

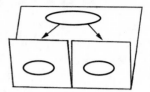

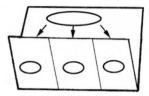

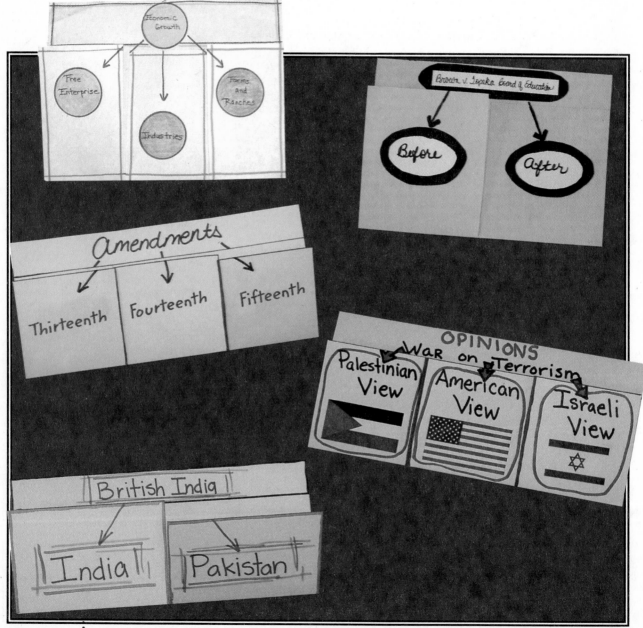

Vocabulary Book

1. Fold a sheet of notebook paper in half like a *hot dog*.

2. On one side, cut every third line. This usually results in ten tabs.

3. Label the tabs. See the illustration below for several uses.

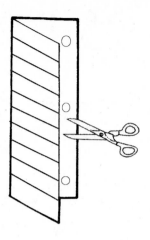

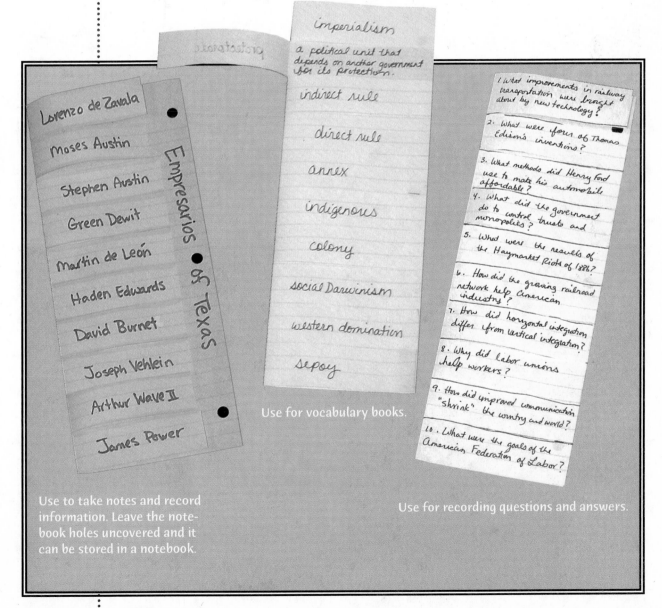

Empresarios ● of Texas

Lorenzo de Zavala

Moses Austin

Stephen Austin

Green Dewit

Martin de León

Haden Edwards

David Burnet

Joseph Vehlein

Arthur Wave II

James Power

imperialism

a political unit that depends on another government for its protection.

indirect rule

direct rule

annex

indigenous

colony

social Darwinism

western domination

sepoy

Use for vocabulary books.

1. What improvements in railway transportation were brought about by new technology?

2. What were four of Thomas Edison's inventions?

3. What methods did Henry Ford use to make his automobile affordable?

4. What did the government do to control trusts and monopolies?

5. What were the results of the Haymarket Riots of 1886?

6. How did the growing railroad network help American industry?

7. How did horizontal integration differ from vertical integration?

8. Why did labor unions help workers?

9. How did improved communication "shrink" the country and world?

10. What were the goals of the American Federation of Labor?

Use for recording questions and answers.

Use to take notes and record information. Leave the notebook holes uncovered and it can be stored in a notebook.

Four-Door Diorama

1. Make a *four-door book* out of a *shutter fold* (p. 21).

2. Fold the two inside corners back to the outer edges *(mountains)* of the *shutter fold*. This will result in two *tacos* that will make the *four-door book* look like it has a shirt collar. Do the same thing to the bottom of the *four-door book*. When finished, four small triangular *tacos* have been made.

3. Form a 90-degree angle and overlap the folded triangles to make a display case that doesn't use staples or glue. (It can be collapsed for storage.)

4. Or, as illustrated, cut off all four triangles, or *tacos*. Staple or glue the sides.

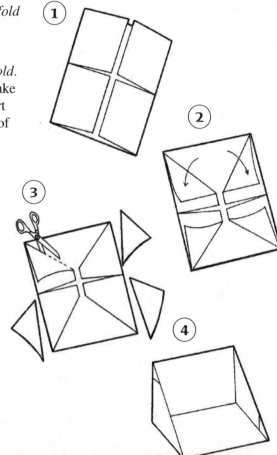

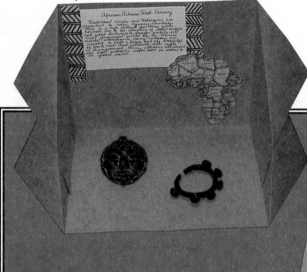

Use 11" × 17" paper to make a large display case.

Use poster board to make giant display cases.

Place display cases next to each other to compare and contrast or to sequence events or data.

Picture Frame Book

1. Fold a sheet of paper in half like a *hamburger.*

2. Open the *hamburger* and gently roll one side of the *hamburger* toward the *valley.* Try not to crease the roll.

3. Cut a rectangle out of the middle of the rolled side of the paper leaving a half-inch border, forming a frame.

4. Fold another sheet of paper in half like a *hamburger.* Apply glue to the inside border of the picture frame and place the folded, uncut sheet of paper inside.

Use this book to feature a person, place, or thing. Inside the picture frames, glue photographs, magazine pictures, computer-generated graphs, or have students sketch pictures. This book has three inside pages for writing and recording notes.

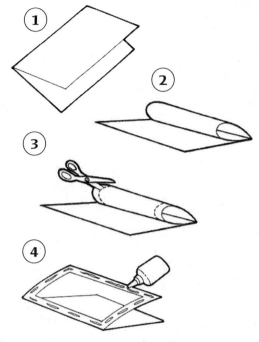

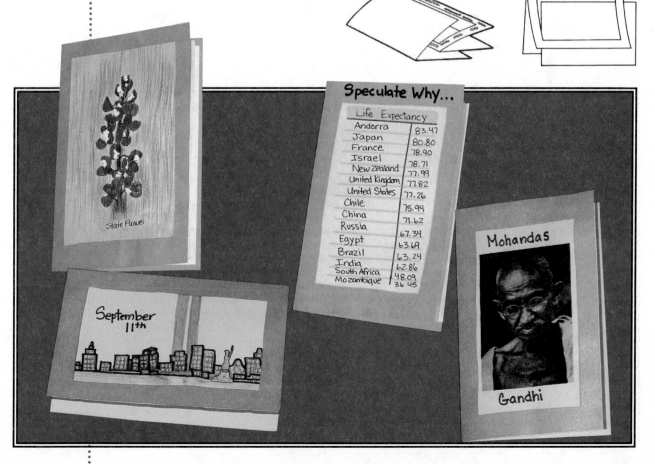

Speculate Why...

Life Expectancy

Andorra	83.47
Japan	80.80
France	78.90
Israel	78.71
New Zealand	77.99
United Kingdom	77.82
United States	77.26
Chile	75.94
China	71.62
Russia	67.34
Egypt	63.69
Brazil	63.24
India	62.86
South Africa	48.09
Mozambique	36.45

State Flower

September 11th

Mohandas
Gandhi

Display Case

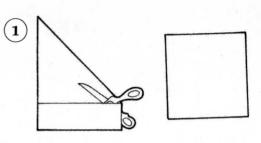

1. Make a *taco* fold and cut off the leftover piece. This will result in a square.

2. Fold the square into a *shutter fold.*

3. Unfold and fold the square into another *shutter fold* perpendicular to the direction of the first. This will form a small square at each of the four corners of the sheet of paper.

4. As illustrated, cut along two fold lines on opposite sides of the large square.

5. Collapse the sides in and glue the tabs to form an open box.

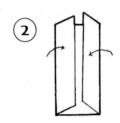

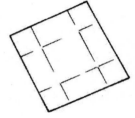

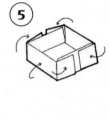

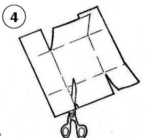

How to Make a Lid

Fold another open-sided box using a square of paper one-half inch larger than the square used to make the first box. This will make a lid that fits snugly over the display box. *Example:* If the base is made out of an $8\frac{1}{2}$" paper square, make the lid out of a 9" square.

Cut a hole out of the lid and cover the opening with a cut piece of acetate used on overhead projectors. Heavy, clear plastic wrap or scraps from a laminating machine will also work. Secure the clear plastic sheet to the inside of the lid with glue or tape.

NOTE: *You can place polystyrene foam or quilt batting in the boxes to display objects. Glue the boxes onto a sheet of cardboard to make them strong enough to display heavy objects.*

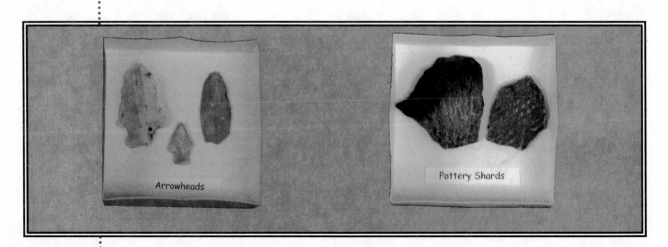

Arrowheads

Pottery Shards

Billboard Project

1. Fold all pieces of the same size of paper in half like *hamburgers*.

2. Place a line of glue at the top and bottom of one side of each folded billboard section and glue them side by side on a larger sheet of paper or poster board. If glued correctly, all doors will open from right to left.

3. Pictures, dates, words, and so on, go on the front of each billboard section. When opened, writing or drawings can be seen on the inside left of each section. The base, or the part glued to the background, is perfect for more in-depth information or definitions.

Use for time lines or for sequencing information, such as events in a war, presidents of the United States, or ratification of states.

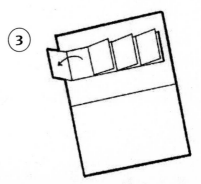

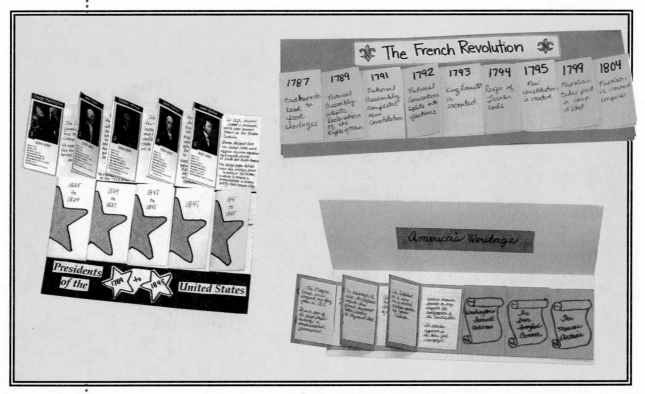

Project Board With Tabs

1. Draw a large illustration, a series of small illustrations, or write on the front of a sheet of paper.

2. Pinch and slightly fold the sheet of paper at the point where a tab is desired on the illustrated sheet of paper. Cut into the paper on the fold. Cut straight in, then cut up to form an "L." When the paper is unfolded, it will form a tab with an illustration on the front.

3. After all tabs have been cut, glue this front sheet onto a second sheet of paper. Place glue around all four edges and in the middle, away from tabs.

Write or draw under the tabs. If the project is made as a bulletin board using butcher paper, tape or glue smaller sheets of paper under the tabs.

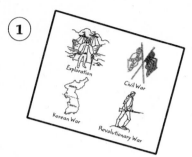

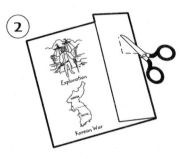

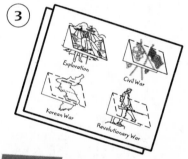

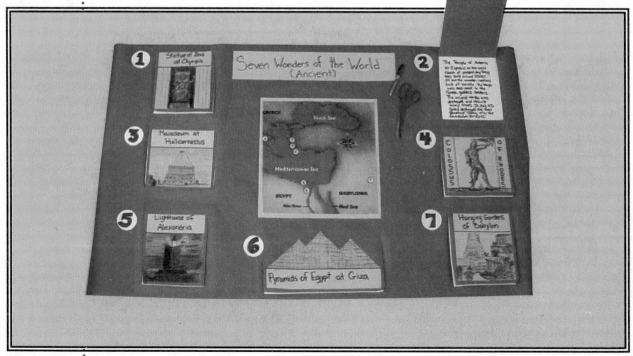

Sentence Strips

1. Take two sheets of paper and fold then into *hamburgers*. Cut along the fold lines making four half sheets. (Use as many half sheets as necessary for additional pages to your book.)

2. Fold each sheet in half like a *hot dog*.

3. Place the folds side by side and staple them together on the left side.

4. One inch from the stapled edge, cut the front page of each folded section up to the *mountain top*. These cuts form flaps that can be raised and lowered.

To make a half-cover, use a sheet of construction paper one inch longer than the book. Glue the back of the last sheet to the construction paper strip leaving one inch on the left side to fold over and cover the original staples. Staple this half-cover in place.

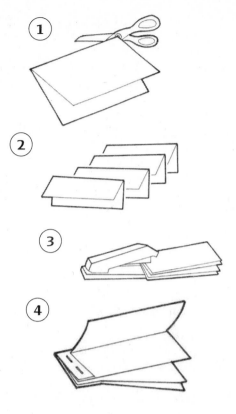

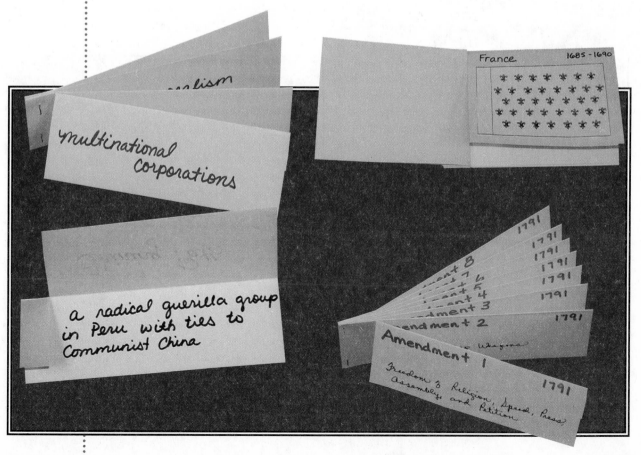

Sentence-Strip Holder

1. Fold a sheet of paper in half like a *hamburger.*

2. Open the *hamburger* and fold the two outer edges toward the *valley*. This forms a *shutter fold.*

3. Fold one of the inside edges of the shutter back to the outside fold. This fold forms a floppy L-tab.

4. Glue the floppy L-tab down to the base so that it forms a strong, straight L-tab.

5. Glue the other shutter side to the front of this L-tab. This forms a tent that is the backboard for the flashcards or student work to be displayed.

6. Fold the edge of the L-tab up one-quarter to one-half inch to form a lip that will keep the student work from slipping off the holder.

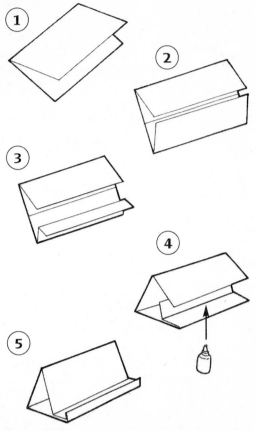

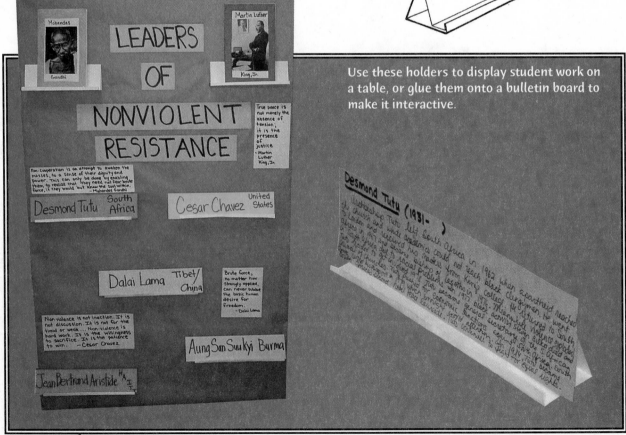

Use these holders to display student work on a table, or glue them onto a bulletin board to make it interactive.

Forward-Backward Book

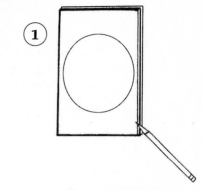

1. Stack three or more sheets of paper. On the top sheet, trace a large circle.

2. With the papers still stacked, cut out the circles.

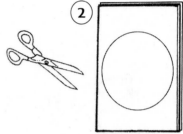

3. Staple the paper circles together along the left-hand side to create a circular booklet.

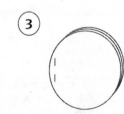

4. Label the cover and takes notes on the pages that open to the right.

5. Turn the book upside down and label the back. Takes notes on the pages that open to the right.

Front

Back

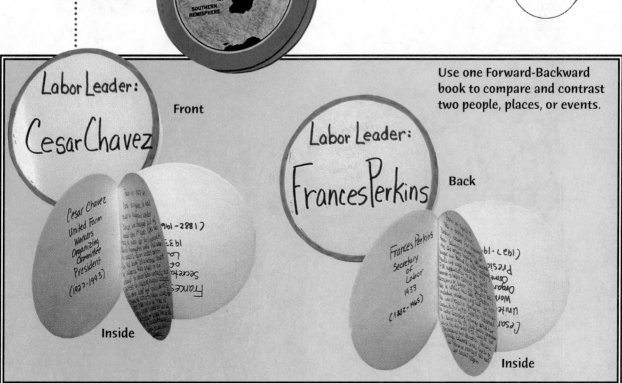

Front

Back

Labor Leader: CesarChavez

Cesar Chavez
United Farm
Workers
Organizing
Committee
President
(1927-1993)

Inside

Labor Leader: FrancesPerkins

Frances Perkins
Secretary
of
Labor
1933
(1882-1965)

Inside

Use one Forward-Backward book to compare and contrast two people, places, or events.

Three-Pocket Book

1. Fold a horizontal sheet of paper (11" × 17") into thirds.

2. Fold the bottom edge up two inches and crease well. Glue the outer edges of the two-inch tab to create three pockets.

3. Label each pocket. Use these pockets to hold notes taken on index cards or quarter sheets of paper.

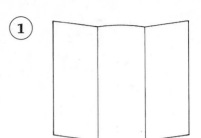

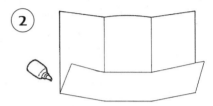

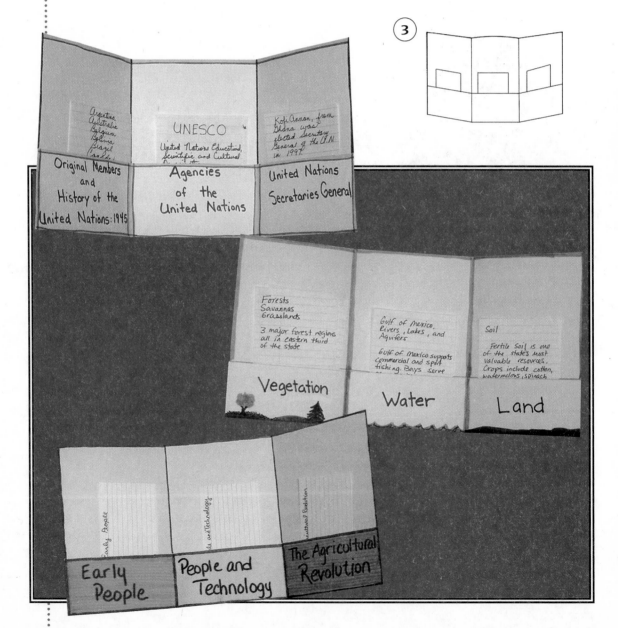

Chapter Activities for

The American Republic
To 1877

The pages that follow contain chapter-specific Foldables activities to use with *The American Republic to 1877*. Included are a Chapter Summary, a reproduction of the Foldables Study Organizer that appears on each chapter opener in the textbook, and a Follow-Up Foldables Activity. Use the Follow-Up Activity after students have studied each chapter. Students are asked to use the Foldables they have created and completed during the study of each chapter to review important chapter concepts and prepare for the chapter test.

Alternative Foldables activities are also included for every chapter. Use these activities during the study of each chapter or as chapter review activities. The Student Study Tip provides reading, writing, and test-taking strategies that you can share with your students throughout the course.

Chapter-Specific

FOLDABLES

The First Americans

CHAPTER SUMMARY

The Inca, Maya, and Aztec societies in South and Central America and in Mexico created powerful empires. Among the most advanced of the early cultures were the Hohokam and Anasazi of the Southwest and the Mound Builders of the Ohio River valley. In the Southwest, Native American peoples improved techniques of irrigation to farm the land. The Great Plains group depended on the great herds of bison, or buffalo, that roamed the plains. Native Americans of the Northeast formed the Iroquois League to solve disputes.

CHAPTER PREVIEW

Categorizing Study Foldable Group information into categories to make sense of what you are learning. Make this foldable to learn about the first Americans.

Step 1 Fold one sheet of paper in half from top to bottom.

Step 2 Fold in half again, from side to side.

Step 3 Unfold the paper once. Cut up the fold of the top flap only.

This cut will make two tabs.

Step 4 Turn the paper vertically and sketch the continents of North and Central and South America on the front tabs.

Reading and Writing As you read the chapter, write under the flaps of your foldable what you learn about the Native American people living in these regions.

CHAPTER REVIEW

Foldables Follow-Up Activity

Once students have created their foldables, review with them the different uses foldables have: self-check quiz, quick chapter review, and group quiz. Then have students organize themselves into small groups to quiz each other about their foldables. Ask students to name two other topics in the chapter that would adapt well to this foldable.

TEACHER NOTES

_____
_____
_____
_____
_____
_____
_____
_____
_____
_____
_____
_____
_____
_____

Alternative Activities for Chapter 1

CAUSE AND EFFECT

Have students use the same foldable design to study about the rise and decline of one of the Native American groups in the chapter. Suggest students add color, shapes, or illustrations to make the information more memorable for them. Ask students to think about what factors could have prevented the decline of each group.

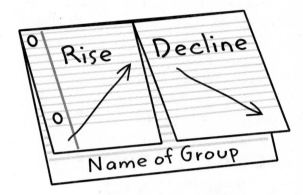

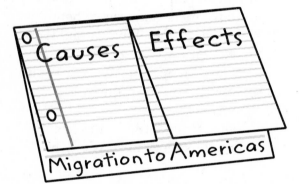

EVALUATING

Suggest students use the same foldable design to help them study the causes and effects of early peoples coming to the Americas. Encourage them to use concise phrases and single-word clues rather than complete sentences. Ask students what geographic element allowed settlement of the Americas. *(Earth's climate)*

Student Study Tip

As they are learning about early Native Americans, suggest to students that it is sometimes difficult to remember what each group was like, especially when they have unfamiliar names. To help them remember, suggest they choose a group characteristic that starts with the same first letter of the group.

Chapter 1 FOLDABLES

Exploring the Americas

CHAPTER SUMMARY

Many explorations took place in the 1400s and 1500s and as early as c. A.D. 1000 when Leif Eriksson landed in present-day Newfoundland. The explorers represented the strongest countries at the time: England, Spain, France and the Netherlands. They were searching for new trade routes and riches. In the late 1400s, Dias, Columbus, and da Gama set sail. Explorers such as Magellan, Cartier, De Soto, and Hudson all followed in the next 50 years. In 1565 Spain established the first settlement at St. Augustine, Florida.

CHAPTER PREVIEW

FOLDABLES™

Study Organizer

Evaluating Information Study Foldable
Make this foldable to help you learn about European exploration of the Americas.

Step 1 Fold the paper from the top right corner down so the edges line up. Cut off the leftover piece.

> Fold a triangle. Cut off the extra edge.

Step 2 Fold the triangle in half. Unfold.

> The folds will form an X dividing four equal sections.

Step 3 Cut up one fold line and stop at the middle. Draw an X on one tab and label the other three.

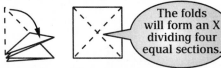

Step 4 Fold the X flap under the other flap and glue together.

> This makes a three-sided pyramid.

Reading and Writing As you read, ask yourself why England, France, and Spain were exploring the Americas. Write your questions under each appropriate pyramid wall.

CHAPTER REVIEW

Foldables Follow-Up Activity

As students complete their foldables about explorers in the Americas, pair them with partners and have them quiz each other about the reasons they wrote down. Have them summarize what they learned, and state the two most valid reasons explorers came to the Americas. Choose groups at random to share with the rest of the class the two reasons they chose as to why explorers came to the Americas.

TEACHER NOTES

_____
_____
_____
_____
_____
_____
_____
_____
_____
_____
_____

Alternative Activities for Chapter 2

DESCRIBING

Have students choose three explorers mentioned in the chapter and do research to find out more about them. Have them write details of the explorer's voyages on the appropriate side of their pyramids. Have them share their research with the class.

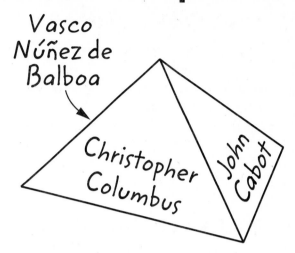

DRAWING CONCLUSIONS

Using the same pyramid foldable design, have students research more about the great early African kingdoms of Ghana, Mali, and Songhai. Once they have completed their research, have them draw conclusions about why each kingdom eventually faded away.

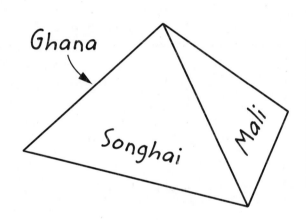

Student Study Tip

As students research the routes of early explorers, or other topics such as military campaigns, suggest they take time to find the specific locations on a map or globe. This will make the information more dimensional and give students some geographic perspective.

Chapter 2 FOLDABLES

Colonial America

CHAPTER SUMMARY

The early North American colonies were a meeting place for many different cultures. People came to the American colonies for various reasons—including the pursuit of wealth, land, or religious freedom. The goals and ways of life of these different groups sometimes clashed, ending in conflict. However, America was becoming a place where people of different backgrounds and beliefs could learn to live together peacefully.

CHAPTER PREVIEW

Comparison Study Foldable When you group facts into categories, it is easier to make comparisons. Make this foldable to compare and contrast the 13 colonies and their regions.

Step 1 Collect 7 sheets of paper and place them about $\frac{1}{2}$ inch apart.

Keep the edges straight.

Step 2 Fold up the bottom edges of the paper to form 14 tabs.

This makes all tabs the same size.

Step 3 When all the tabs are the same size, crease the paper to hold the tabs in place and staple the sheets together. Label each tab with the name of a colony and color-code each region.

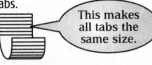

Staple together along the fold.

The Thirteen Colonies	
Massachusetts	Northern
New Hampshire	
Rhode Island	
Connecticut	
New York	Middle
Delaware	
New Jersey	
Pennsylvania	
Virginia	Southern
Maryland	
North Carolina	
South Carolina	
Georgia	

Reading and Writing As you read, write what you learn about each of the 13 colonies under each tab and compare the colonies.

CHAPTER REVIEW

Foldables Follow-Up Activity

Have students create a matching quiz of 10 questions using information from their foldables. Then ask students to trade quizzes with a classmate and see how many questions they can answer correctly. Ask for several volunteers to write their quizzes on the board for everyone to try.

TEACHER NOTES

_____

_____

_____

_____

_____

_____

_____

_____

_____

_____

_____

_____

_____

_____

_____

Alternative Activities for Chapter 3

SEQUENCING

Have students use the same foldable design to create a time line that shows key events in the founding of the settlements of Jamestown, Plymouth, and Massachusetts Bay. Have them draw rough maps pinpointing each location.

Early English Settlements
Jamestown
Plymouth
Massachusetts Bay

Summary of What I've Learned
New England Colonies
Middle Colonies
Southern Colonies

EVALUATING

Ask students to imagine they are new settlers who are traveling throughout the 13 colonies before they decide where to live. Ask them to list on the foldable the best things and the worst things about living in each of the regions. Then ask students to write a statement identifying their choice and describing their feelings about their new home.

Student Study Tip

To help students grasp the main ideas, have them create a word web as they read each section. Direct students to write the section title as the center of the web; for example, "Section 3: Middle Colonies." Tell students to include important ideas in ovals around the center.

Chapter 3 FOLDABLES

The Colonies Grow

CHAPTER SUMMARY

Colonists brought traditions from their home countries and developed new ways of life in America. Many people made important contributions. A number of languages, foods from many lands, and a variety of religious beliefs and holidays all became part of the emerging culture of colonial America. While lifestyles varied from region to region, in time the colonists found that they shared many concerns. The ideals of American democracy and freedom of religion took root during the colonial period.

CHAPTER PREVIEW

Compare-Contrast Study Foldable Make the following (Venn diagram) foldable to compare and contrast the peoples involved in the French and Indian War.

Step 1 Fold a sheet of paper from side to side, leaving a 2-inch tab uncovered along the side.

Fold it so the left edge lies 2 inches from the right edge.

Step 2 Turn the paper and fold into thirds.

Step 3 Unfold and cut along the two inside fold lines.

Cut along the two folds on the front flap to make 3 tabs.

Step 4 Label the foldable as shown.

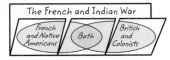

The French and Indian War

French and Native Americans | Both | British and Colonists

Reading and Writing As you read about the participants of the war, write facts about them under the appropriate tabs of your foldable.

CHAPTER REVIEW

Foldables Follow-Up Activity

Once students have created their foldables, have them identify the causes and effects of the French and Indian War for the various people who lived in the Americas. Have them share their information with the class. Prompt students to develop a consensus based on the class discussion.

TEACHER NOTES

_____
_____
_____
_____
_____
_____
_____
_____
_____
_____
_____
_____
_____
_____
_____

Alternative Activities for Chapter 4

COMPARING

Using the same Venn diagram foldable design, have students research to find out more about the colonial economy. Ask them to compare farming in New England with farming in the Southern Colonies among other things.

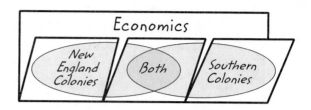

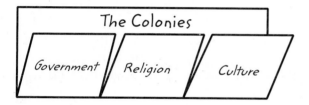

IDENTIFYING

Have students write *Government, Religion,* and *Culture* on their foldables. Under each of the categories, have students identify at least two key events or facts from the colonial period. For each event or fact, ask them to explain its significance. Discuss the students' foldables as a class.

Student Study Tip

Point out that understanding cause and effect is essential to studying history. Students must know not only what happened, but why it happened. Note that most effects have more than one cause and that causes can have more than one effect. Show students several examples of cause-and-effect charts.

Chapter 4 FOLDABLES

Road to Independence

CHAPTER SUMMARY

Before the 1770s, most people in the American colonies thought of themselves as British citizens. Few wanted or expected any major changes in their relationships with the king or with Parliament. However, those feelings of loyalty were changing. As Britain imposed a number of taxes on the colonies, tension grew between the two sides. When colonial objections to British law could no longer be settled by protests or petitions to the king, war and the colonies' final break with Britain followed.

CHAPTER PREVIEW

FOLDABLES™
Study Organizer

Cause-and-Effect Study Foldable Make this foldable to show the causes and effects of the events that led the Americans to declare independence from Great Britain.

Step 1 Fold one sheet of paper in half from side to side.

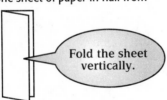

Fold the sheet vertically.

Step 2 Fold again, 1 inch from the top. (**Tip:** The middle knuckle of your index finger is about 1 inch long.)

Step 3 Open and label as shown.

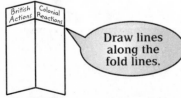

British Actions | Colonial Reactions

Draw lines along the fold lines.

Reading and Writing As you read this chapter, fill in the causes (British Actions) and effects (Colonial Reactions) in the correct columns of your foldable.

CHAPTER REVIEW

Foldables Follow-Up Activity

After students have completed their foldables, call on volunteers to share their entries with the rest of the class. Have students note the events that appear most often in the entries. Then arrange a class debate where half the class represents the British government and the other half represents American colonists. They should try to give reasons for each cause and effect, respectively.

TEACHER NOTES

_____
_____
_____
_____
_____
_____
_____
_____
_____
_____
_____
_____

Alternative Activities for Chapter 5

IDENTIFYING

Ask students to identify important actions taken by the First Continental Congress and by the Second Continental Congress. Students should write these on their foldables. Then have them organize themselves into small groups and explain why they think the two congresses took these actions.

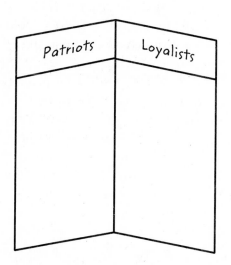

EVALUATING

On their foldables, have students list at least three reasons why a Patriot might support independence and three reasons why a Loyalist might support allegiance to Britain. Suggest that students single out what they think is the most important reason.

Student Study Tip

Stress that students should read any assigned work before attending class. Lectures and discussions will make more sense, and they will be able to relate the ideas discussed in class to what they have read before class. Tell students that taking notes in their own words as they read the assignment can help sharpen their attention and concentration.

Chapter 5 FOLDABLES

The American Revolution

CHAPTER SUMMARY

The American colonies declared their independence in 1776, but no country recognized it as an independent nation until after the Revolutionary War ended in 1783. The war between the Patriots—Americans who supported independence, and the Loyalists—those who remained loyal to Britain, was a people's movement. The Patriot victory at Yorktown convinced the British that the war was too costly to pursue. In 1783 the Treaty of Paris was signed, marking the end of the revolution. Great Britain recognized the United States as an independent nation.

CHAPTER PREVIEW

FOLDABLES™
Study Organizer

Organizing Information Study Foldable
When you group information into categories on a table, it is easier to compare characteristics of items. Make this foldable to help you compare the attitudes and actions of the Patriots and Loyalists.

Step 1 Fold a sheet of paper into thirds from top to bottom.

This forms three rows.

Step 2 Open the paper and refold it into fourths from side to side.

Fold it in half, then in half again.

This forms four columns.

Step 3 Unfold, turn the paper, and draw lines along the folds.

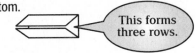

Step 4 Label your table as shown.

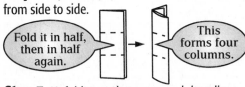

The American Revolution	Patriots	Loyalists
Beginning		
Middle		
End		

Reading and Writing As you read about the American Revolution, write down facts about the attitudes and actions of the Patriots and Loyalists at different times during the war.

CHAPTER REVIEW

Foldables Follow-Up Activity

Organize students into small groups, and have them role play the Patriots and Loyalists at different times during the war. Suggest that they use their foldable answers to help them perform the role play. As a class, discuss the role play choices. If you have extra time, have the students switch sides so they can see things from both perspectives.

TEACHER NOTES

_____

_____

_____

_____

_____

_____

_____

_____

_____

_____

_____

_____

_____

Alternative Activities for Chapter 6

CAUSE AND EFFECT

Have students make a foldable to determine the causes and effects of the Declaration of Independence, the French and American Alliance, and the Treaty of Paris. Organize students into pairs so they can compare answers and learn from each other.

Revolutionary War	Cause	Effect
Declaration of Independence		
French and American Alliance		
Treaty of Paris		

Revolutionary War	Who	What
George Washington		
Abigail Adams		
Lord Cornwallis		

CATEGORIZING

Have students make a foldable that lists three people from the chapter. In one column, students should write who they were, and in the second column, they should identify several contributions made by each individual. In small groups, have students guess who the famous person is from each student's descriptions.

Student Study Tip

As students are learning about the Revolutionary War, help them remember the differences between the Patriots and the Loyalists by creating a short rhyme or jingle about each group that includes interesting, identifiable facts. Students may work in pairs or individually. Ask for volunteers to share their rhymes with the class.

Chapter 6 FOLDABLES

A More Perfect Union

CHAPTER SUMMARY

The leaders of the new United States worked to define the powers of government. The Articles of Confederation, America's first constitution, provided for a new central government under which the states gave up little of their power. A new constitution, however, corrected the weaknesses of government under the Articles of Confederation. The United States system of government rests on the Constitution, and also limits the power of government.

CHAPTER PREVIEW

Compare-Contrast Study Foldable Make this foldable to help you compare the Articles of Confederation to the U.S. Constitution.

Step 1 Fold a sheet of paper from side to side, leaving a 2-inch tab uncovered along the side.

Fold it so the left edge lies 2 inches from the right edge.

Step 2 Turn the paper and fold it into thirds.

Step 3 Unfold and cut along the two inside fold lines.

Cut along the two folds on the front flap to make 3 tabs.

Step 4 Label the foldable as shown.

A More Perfect Union

Articles of Confederation | Both | U.S. Constitution

Reading and Writing As you read the chapter, write what you learn about these documents under the appropriate tabs.

CHAPTER REVIEW

Foldables Follow-Up Activity

Once students have completed their foldables, organize them into pairs or small groups. Have each pair or group create a poster using the information from the foldables. Suggest that the students draw pictures, write captions, create titles, and so on. Have each pair or group present their poster to the class. Allow students to ask each other questions about the posters.

TEACHER NOTES

Alternative Activities for Chapter 7

DECISION MAKING

Have students compare the Virginia Plan and the New Jersey Plan with a Venn diagram foldable. Remind students to write characteristics unique to each plan in individual circles. Shared characteristics should be placed in the center of the diagram. Plan a class discussion in which students choose which plan they think is a better one.

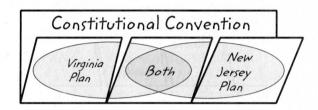

MAKING COMPARISONS

Suggest students use a Venn diagram foldable to compare state powers and national powers of the federal system. Have them write shared powers in the center. Randomly choose students to share specific details about state and national powers, and which level they think has the most power.

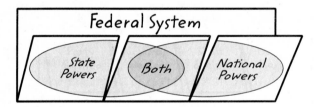

Student Study Tip

As students are learning about the Articles of Confederation and the Constitution, suggest they take time to read the full text of the Constitution on pages 232–253 in their textbooks. It is helpful for students to see the document in front of them when they are learning about it. Remind students that the Constitution has been the fundamental law of the United States for more than 200 years.

Chapter 7 FOLDABLES

A New Nation

CHAPTER SUMMARY

The new government established by George Washington's administration struggled to keep peace at home and to avoid war abroad. Some early challenges included serious financial problems and the Whiskey Rebellion. By the election of 1796, two distinct political parties with different views about the role of the national government had formed—the Federalists and the Democratic-Republicans. Federalists promoted a strong federal government and Democratic-Republicans wanted to limit the federal government's power.

CHAPTER REVIEW

Summarizing Study Foldable Make this foldable and use it as a journal to help you record the major events that occurred as the new nation of the United States formed.

Step 1 Fold a sheet of paper from top to bottom.

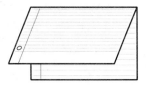

Step 2 Then fold it in half from side to side.

Step 3 Label the foldable as shown.

Journal of American Firsts

Reading and Writing As you read the chapter, find the "firsts" experienced by the new nation, and record them in your foldable journal. For example, list the precedents set by President Washington and identify the first political parties.

CHAPTER REVIEW

Foldables Follow-Up Activity

Have students use their foldables to write questions for an interview with someone prominent from the chapter. Have them write questions about the "firsts" of the new nation. Encourage students to use the information on their foldables to write the questions. Then organize the class into pairs for mock interviews.

TEACHER NOTES

_____
_____
_____
_____
_____
_____
_____
_____
_____
_____
_____
_____

Alternative Activities for Chapter 8

ORGANIZING

Have students research the first political parties and write each party's views inside the first fold of the foldables. Then have students open their foldables to a full-size sheet of paper and write the views of each party leader—Alexander Hamilton and Thomas Jefferson—in separate boxes. Organize the class into two teams. Have students from one team read facts from their foldables out loud and have the other team identify the correct leader or party.

SEQUENCING

Have students identify and write the challenges of the new nation on their foldables. Suggest that students list the early challenges and the results. Then have students draw a time line of the events and highlight the year the events occurred using a colored marker or pen.

Student Study Tip

As students read the chapter, have them take notes about important events, historical dates, and so on, to create an outline. Explain to them that the purpose of an outline is to condense a subject by writing the main ideas in a logical order. This makes the material less overwhelming.

Chapter 8 FOLDABLES

The Jefferson Era

CHAPTER SUMMARY

The election of Thomas Jefferson as the third president marked the transfer of power from one political party to another through a democratic election. Jefferson believed that a large federal government threatened liberty so he reduced the size of the army and navy and eliminated certain taxes to decrease the power of federal government. The Louisiana Purchase opened a vast area to exploration and settlement. Beginning in 1812, the United States was at war with Britain. The end of this war produced a new spirit of nationalism.

CHAPTER PREVIEW

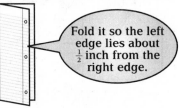

FOLDABLES™
Study Organizer

Organizing Information Study Foldable
Make this foldable to organize information and sequence events about the Jefferson era into a flowchart.

Step 1 Fold a sheet of paper in half from side to side.

Fold it so the left edge lies about $\frac{1}{2}$ inch from the right edge.

Step 2 Turn the paper and fold it into thirds.

Step 3 Unfold and cut the top layer only along both folds. Then cut each of the three tabs in half.

This will make six tabs.

Step 4 Label your foldable as shown.

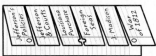

Reading and Writing As you read, select key facts about the events of the Jefferson era and write them under the tabs of your foldable.

CHAPTER REVIEW

Foldables Follow-Up Activity

Organize students into small groups to discuss the events of the Jefferson Era. Suggest they create a trivia game with the information from their foldables. Have them create a scoring system as well. Then have students switch groups to play their trivia games.

TEACHER NOTES

_____

_____

_____

_____

_____

_____

_____

_____

_____

_____

_____

Alternative Activities for Chapter 9

DEFINING

Have students create a mini vocabulary book with key terms and places from the chapter. They may choose terms at random or go section by section. Have them write the terms and places on the outside tabs with definitions under the foldable tabs. Encourage students to use bright markers and pens to make their mini books more memorable.

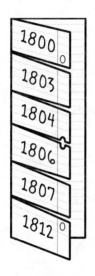

ORGANIZING

Have students create a mini book of important dates during the Jefferson Era. Tell students to choose dates in chronological order and list them on the outside of their foldables. Underneath the tabs, have students list the significant event that occurred on that date. Ask students at random to share with the class why they chose the dates and events they did.

Student Study Tip

As students read the chapter, have them create an information bank at the beginning of each section in their notes. Suggest students ask themselves questions about what they think they will learn in each section. Then suggest they go back after class lectures and discussion to fill in what they learned.

Chapter 9 **FOLDABLES**

Growth and Expansion

CHAPTER SUMMARY

The rise of industry and trade in the United States led to an Industrial Revolution that caused major growth of cities. The huge amount of territory added to the United States during the early 1800s gave the country a large store of natural resources and provided land for more settlers. As the nation grew, differences in economic activities and needs increased sectionalism. The Monroe Doctrine was announced in 1823, which opposed colonization and set the groundwork for America's foreign policy stance.

CHAPTER PREVIEW

Cause-and-Effect Study Foldable Make this foldable to help you analyze the causes and effects of growth in the East and expansion into the West of the United States.

Step 1 Fold one sheet of paper in half from top to bottom.

Step 2 Fold it in half again, from side to side.

Step 3 Unfold the paper once. Sketch an outline of the United States across both tabs and label them as shown.

Step 4 Cut up the fold of the top flap only.

This cut will make two tabs.

Reading and Writing As you read the chapter, list causes and effects of eastern growth and western expansion under the appropriate tabs of your foldable.

CHAPTER REVIEW

Foldables Follow-Up Activity

To help students better understand cause and effect, try the following activity. In small groups, have one student be the spokesperson who reads either a cause or an effect out loud. The other students in the group should quickly identify if the statement is a cause or an effect. Have students take turns being the spokesperson so everyone can share their foldable.

TEACHER NOTES

_____
_____
_____
_____
_____
_____
_____
_____
_____
_____
_____
_____
_____

Alternative Activities for Chapter 10

CAUSE AND EFFECT

Ask students to create a foldable with a partner. Have students look through the chapter to find causes and effects of industrialization. Encourage students to discuss the benefits of industrialization, and how things are different today. Display the foldables on a bulletin board.

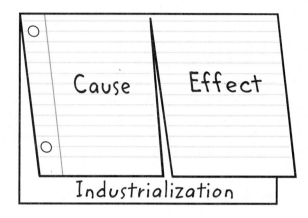

ANALYZING

Have students create foldables about the pros and cons of moving west. Organize the class into two groups. Instruct one half of the class to present the pros and the other to present the cons. Then have the two groups debate whether to move west or not.

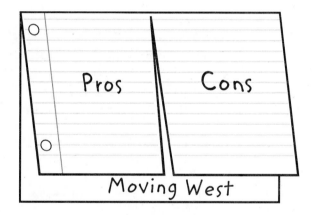

Student Study Tip

As students read the chapter, remind them that picture clues can help them remember information. Have students choose themes in the chapter that can be represented with a picture. Students may want to draw a rough sketch of the pictures as part of their note taking to help them remember key concepts.

Chapter 10 FOLDABLES

The Jackson Era

CHAPTER SUMMARY

Americans, for the first time, elected a president from the nation's frontier—Andrew Jackson. More people were able to take part in politics because of an expansion of suffrage and changes in political practice. The political gains, however, did not extend to women, Native Americans, and African Americans. As more white settlers moved into the Southeast, conflict arose between the Native Americans who lived there and the United States government. Economic issues affected the presidencies of Jackson and Van Buren.

CHAPTER PREVIEW

FOLDABLES™
Study Organizer

Evaluating Information Study Foldable
Make this foldable to help you ask and answer questions about the Jackson era.

Step 1 Fold a sheet of paper in half from side to side, leaving a $\frac{1}{2}$ inch tab along the side.

Leave $\frac{1}{2}$ inch tab here.

Step 2 Turn the paper and fold it into fourths.

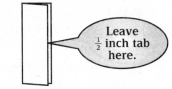

Fold in half, then fold in half again.

Step 3 Unfold and cut up along the three fold lines.

Make four tabs.

Step 4 Label your foldable as shown.

Who? What? When? Why?

Reading and Writing As you read, ask yourself "who" Andrew Jackson was, "what" he did, "when" he did it, and "why" it happened. Write your thoughts and facts under each appropriate tab.

CHAPTER REVIEW

Foldables Follow-Up Activity

Have students debate whether they support or oppose the following statement: Andrew Jackson's presidency ushered in a new age in American government and politics. Encourage students to use the information compiled in their foldables to support their positions.

TEACHER NOTES

_____
_____
_____
_____
_____
_____
_____
_____
_____
_____
_____
_____

Alternative Activities for Chapter 11

IDENTIFYING OPTIONS

Point out that many whites during this era coveted the lands of Native Americans. Because of this, some state governments forcibly removed the Native Americans from those lands. Have students write *Cherokee Nation, Seminole People,* and *Sauk and Fox People* on the outside tabs of their foldables. Ask students to write what actions these groups took to resist removal under the appropriate tabs.

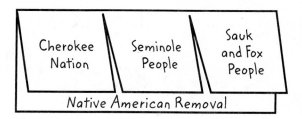

SEQUENCING

Tell students that many important events took place during the 1830s and 1840s. Have students choose four significant years from the chapter to write on the outside of their foldables. Then have them list at least one event and the significance under each tab. Hold a class discussion until all important years are covered.

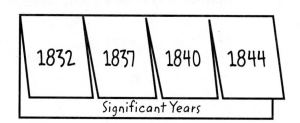

Student Study Tip

Point out that political cartoonists use pictures to present their opinions about issues. They often use symbols like Uncle Sam to represent something else. Have students analyze the cartoons in Chapter 11. What symbols are used? What ideas are the cartoonists presenting? This will help students understand other's viewpoints.

Manifest Destiny

Tremendous expansion during the first half of the 1800s left a lasting imprint on the United States. Manifest Destiny is the idea that the United States was meant to extend its borders from the Atlantic Ocean to the Pacific Ocean. Americans moved west into Texas, New Mexico, California, and the Oregon country. Texas gained its independence from Mexico. Because of American expansion into the Spanish Southwest, tension between the United States and Mexico began to build. Victory in a war with Mexico, along with purchases and treaty agreements, eventually resulted in the United States stretching from the Atlantic Ocean to the Pacific Ocean.

CHAPTER PREVIEW

FOLDABLES™
Study Organizer

Organizing Information Study Foldable
Make this foldable to organize information from the chapter to help you learn more about how Manifest Destiny led to western expansion.

Step 1 Collect three sheets of paper and place them on top of one another about 1 inch apart.

Keep the edges straight.

Step 2 Fold up the bottom edges of the paper to form 6 tabs.

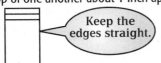

This makes all tabs the same size.

Step 3 When all the tabs are the same size, fold the paper to hold the tabs in place and staple the sheets together. Turn the paper and label each tab as shown.

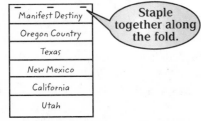

Manifest Destiny
Oregon Country
Texas
New Mexico
California
Utah

Staple together along the fold.

Reading and Writing As you read, use your foldable to write under each appropriate tab what you learn about Manifest Destiny and how it affected the borders of the United States.

CHAPTER REVIEW

Foldables Follow-Up Activity
Have students use their finished foldables to answer the following questions: Why did Americans settle in territories outside the United States? How did white Americans justify taking land from Native Americans and Mexico? What might have occurred had opponents of Manifest Destiny been in the White House? After students have answered the questions individually, have them get into small groups to discuss their answers.

TEACHER NOTES
_____
_____
_____
_____
_____
_____
_____
_____
_____
_____

Alternative Activities for Chapter 12

DESCRIBING

Ask students to scan the chapter to identify five individuals they would like to know more about. Have them list one person on each tab of their foldable. Using information from the chapter and from other sources, students should describe important events in each person's life. Ask them to share their information with the rest of the class.

Biography

CATEGORIZING

Have students label the five tabs of their foldables with the following: *Mexico Gains Independence, Manifest Destiny Attitudes, Polk's War Plan, Capture of Mexico City,* and *Peace Treaty.* Under each tab, have students write two quiz questions. For example, under *Mexico Gains Independence,* ask: From what country did Mexico win its independence? What happened to Spain's mission system? Have volunteers ask their questions to the other students.

War With Mexico
Mexico Gains Independence
Manifest Destiny Attitudes
Polk's War Plan
Capture of Mexico City
Peace Treaty

Student Study Tip

To help students understand primary sources, ask them to write a diary entry covering their trip to school today. Suggest that they write what they saw, whom they encountered, and their expectations for the day. Then have students consider how such diary entries might be of use to historians.

Chapter 12 **FOLDABLES**

North and South

CHAPTER SUMMARY

The North and South developed distinctly different ways of life. The North developed a manufacturing economy that rivaled industrial Europe. Life in the industrial North was hard for many workers as they toiled long hours for low pay in dangerous factories. Instead of manufacturing, the South's economy was based on agriculture. Wealthy plantation owners ruled over much of Southern society, while poor whites and enslaved Africans lived hard lives.

CHAPTER PREVIEW

Compare-and-Contrast Study Foldable
Make this foldable to help you analyze the similarities and differences between the development of the North and the South.

Step 1 Mark the midpoint of the side edge of a sheet of paper.

Draw a mark at the midpoint.

Step 2 Turn the paper and fold the outside edges in to touch at the midpoint.

Step 3 Turn and label your foldable as shown.

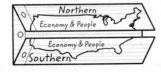

Northern
Economy & People
Economy & People
Southern

Reading and Writing As you read the chapter, collect and write information under the appropriate tab that will help you compare and contrast the people and economics of the Northern and Southern states.

CHAPTER REVIEW

Foldables Follow-Up Activity
Have students make posters in small groups using the information in their foldables. Students should choose either the North or South, sketch a map, and draw symbols in bright colors that are representative of each area. For example, they could draw factories, strike signs, and ships for the North. For the South, they could draw cotton, plantation homes, and farms.

TEACHER NOTES

_____

_____

_____

_____

_____

_____

_____

_____

_____

_____

_____

_____

Alternative Activities for Chapter 13

COMPARING

Tell students to make foldables to compare the lives of African American workers in a Northern factory and enslaved African Americans in the South. Suggest that students use categories such as "How were their lives different?" and "How were their lives similar?"

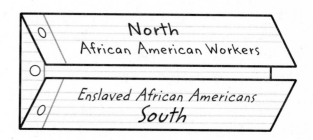

EXPLAINING

Have students select one technological advance that aided the industrial and manufacturing boom in the North and one advance that aided the agricultural boom in the South. Ask students to research to find information about how the technologies were developed and what benefits they provided. They should write this information on their foldables.

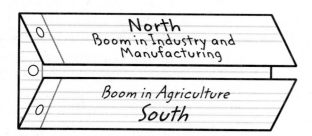

Student Study Tip

Point out that the first word in a question signals the task that is required to successfully answer it. Words such as "List" or "Identify" emphasize information collection. Other words call for description like "Describe" or "Explain." Still others ask students to compare and contrast. Ask students to look through the questions in Chapter 13 and discuss the kinds of responses required.

Chapter 13 FOLDABLES

The Age of Reform

CHAPTER SUMMARY

In the early 1800s, many religious and social reformers attempted to improve American life and education and help people with disabilities. The Second Great Awakening, a new religious movement, inspired people to become involved in missionary work and social reform movements. Abolitionists like William Lloyd Garrison and Frederick Douglass worked to end slavery. Suffragists struggled for equal rights for women. While religious and social reformers fought to change society, writers and painters explored the relationship between humans and nature.

CHAPTER PREVIEW

FOLDABLES™
Study Organizer

Identifying Main Ideas Study Foldable
Make and use this foldable to identify and describe major topics about the Age of Reform.

Step 1 Fold the paper from the top right corner down so the edges line up. Cut off the leftover piece.

> Fold a triangle. Cut off the extra edge.

Step 2 Fold the triangle in half. Unfold.

> The folds will form an X dividing four equal sections.

Step 3 Cut up one fold and stop at the middle. Draw an X on one tab and label the other three as shown.

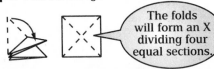

Step 4 Fold the X flap under the other flap and glue together.

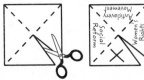

> This makes a three-sided pyramid.

Reading and Writing As you read, write what you learn about social reform, the antislavery movement, and the women's rights movement under each appropriate pyramid wall.

CHAPTER REVIEW

Foldables Follow-Up Activity

Once students have created their foldables, ask them to choose a type of reform from the chapter that interests them and research to find the most current information about it. For example, what are the basic principles of public education today? Are children required to attend school? Students should combine all of their research onto a poster board to show the "Then v. Now" aspect of their reform.

TEACHER NOTES

_____
_____
_____
_____
_____
_____
_____
_____
_____
_____
_____
_____
_____

Alternative Activities for Chapter 14

IDENTIFYING

Tell students to select and research a historical figure mentioned in Chapter 14. Have them write *Who*, *What*, and *When* on each side of their pyramid foldables, and ask them to fill in the information that they have learned in the respective spaces on the foldable. Have students share their work with a partner.

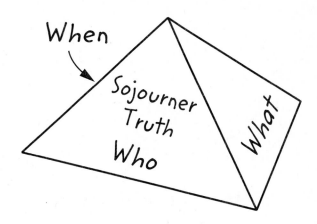

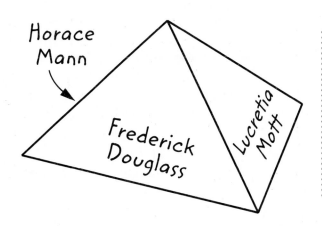

DESCRIBING

Have students choose three people from the chapter to write on each side of their pyramid foldables. Under each name, or inside the foldable, they should write the contributions of each. Ask for volunteers to share their foldables with the rest of the class so the important people in the chapter are discussed.

Student Study Tip

As students read about the reforms of the early nineteenth century, remind them that reform occurs when there are problems in society. Help students create a Problem-Solution Chart with problems from the chapter in one column and the reform established to help solve that problem in the opposite column. They will then have a better understanding of why change is often necessary.

Chapter 14 FOLDABLES

Road to Civil War

CHAPTER SUMMARY

As new states entered the Union, the question of whether to admit them as free states or slave states arose. As Northerners and Southerners grew farther apart, differences could not be solved by compromise. Eager to encourage settlement of the West and to satisfy both the North and the South, Congress passed the Kansas-Nebraska Act, which allowed settlers in each of these two territories to vote on whether to allow slavery. Lincoln's election as president was followed by Southern states leaving the Union. Soon after, the Civil War began.

CHAPTER PREVIEW

Sequencing Events Study Foldable Make and use this foldable to sequence some of the key events that led to the Civil War.

Step 1 Fold a sheet of paper in half from side to side, leaving a $\frac{1}{2}$ inch tab along the side.

Leave $\frac{1}{2}$ inch tab here.

Step 2 Turn the paper and fold it into fourths.

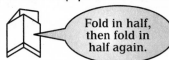

Fold in half, then fold in half again.

Step 3 Unfold and cut up along the three fold lines.

Make four tabs.

Step 4 Label your foldable as shown.

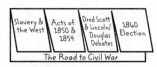

| Slavery & the West | Acts of 1850 & 1854 | Dred Scott & Lincoln/ Douglas Debates | 1860 Election |

The Road to Civil War

Reading and Writing As you read, write facts about the events under each appropriate tab of your foldable. How did these events lead to the Civil War?

CHAPTER REVIEW

Foldables Follow-Up Activity

Once students have created their foldables, have them create a 10-question quiz using the information on their foldables. Ask students to trade quizzes with a classmate. Have them share questions they thought were difficult, and write them on the board for discussion. Offer bonus points to volunteers who would like to research the challenging questions and report back to the class.

TEACHER NOTES

_____
_____
_____
_____
_____
_____
_____
_____
_____
_____
_____

Alternative Activities for Chapter 15

ANALYZING

Have students create foldables to help them understand several events that occurred in the 1850s and how the events may have affected each other. They could choose events from the chapter or label their foldables as shown. Have them list facts under the appropriate tab. Discuss as a class how certain events led to the nation dividing.

1850 Fugitive Slave Act	1852 Uncle Tom's Cabin published	1854 Kansas-Nebraska Act	1856 "Bleeding Kansas"

A Nation Dividing

1854 Republican Party formed	1856 James Buchanan elected	1857 Dred Scott decision	1859 John Brown/ Harper's Ferry

Challenges to Slavery

SUMMARIZING

Have students write the following events on the outside of their foldables: *Republican Party formed; James Buchanan elected; Dred Scott decision,* and *John Brown/Harper's Ferry.* On the inside of their foldables, tell students to summarize how these events challenged slavery. Have them note the final outcome along the inside bottom of their foldables.

Student Study Tip

As students are learning about the tensions that divided the Union, it is important for them to be able to identify the events that led to the South's secession. Students should be able to analyze information by identifying cause-and-effect relationships. Help students identify various causes discussed in the chapter, and then have them list the effects.

Chapter 15 FOLDABLES

The Civil War

CHAPTER SUMMARY

Several Southern states formed the Confederacy when they seceded from the Union. Both the North and the South had strengths and weaknesses that helped determine their military strategies in the Civil War. Neither side gained a strong advantage during the early years of the war. The Union troops failed to take Richmond, which was the Confederate capital at the time. In 1863, however, the North began to win key battles such as Gettysburg and Vicksburg. In April 1865, Lee surrendered to Grant to end the Civil War, giving the victory to the Union.

CHAPTER PREVIEW

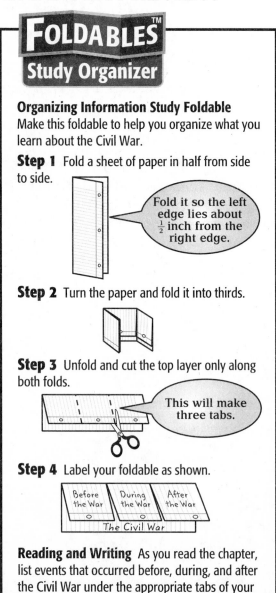

FOLDABLES™
Study Organizer

Organizing Information Study Foldable
Make this foldable to help you organize what you learn about the Civil War.

Step 1 Fold a sheet of paper in half from side to side.

Fold it so the left edge lies about $\frac{1}{2}$ inch from the right edge.

Step 2 Turn the paper and fold it into thirds.

Step 3 Unfold and cut the top layer only along both folds.

This will make three tabs.

Step 4 Label your foldable as shown.

Before the War | During the War | After the War
The Civil War

Reading and Writing As you read the chapter, list events that occurred before, during, and after the Civil War under the appropriate tabs of your foldable.

CHAPTER REVIEW

Foldables Follow-Up Activity

Have each student find a partner. Working together with their completed foldables, have each set of partners create an illustrated time line of the events that occurred before, during, and after the Civil War. Encourage students to be creative by using different kinds of paper, colored markers or pencils, and pictures to illustrate important events.

TEACHER NOTES

_____
_____
_____
_____
_____
_____
_____
_____
_____
_____
_____
_____
_____

Alternative Activities for Chapter 16

EXPLAINING

Have students label their foldables with the following leaders: *Robert E. Lee, William Sherman,* and *Ulysses Grant.* As they read the chapter, they should note roles, contributions, and successes of the leaders and write these under the appropriate tab. Discuss the leaders as a class, and ask students who they found most interesting.

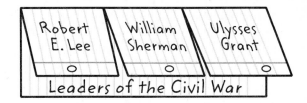

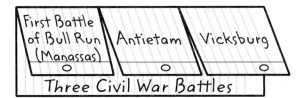

ORGANIZING

Have students select three Civil War battles to research and write the information they find on their foldables. Advise students to include dates and locations of each battle, the military leaders involved, the significance of the battle, the outcome, and so on. Organize the class into groups of four or five, and have the students in each group take turns reading details about a battle out loud until the other students in the group are able to guess which battle is being described.

Student Study Tip

To remember Civil War battles and dates, students could create flashcards which serve as a quick reference and study guide. Have students create interesting cards with mini maps or sketches, and then have them use the cards in groups to study for the chapter test.

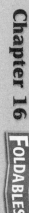

Chapter 16 FOLDABLES

Reconstruction and Its Aftermath

CHAPTER SUMMARY

After the Civil War, Americans attempted to reunite the shattered nation. Differences over how Reconstruction should be carried out divided the government. By the end of 1865, all the former Confederate states had formed new governments and were ready to rejoin the Union. The South worked to rebuild not only its farms and roads, but also its social and political structures. Democrats steadily regained control of Southern governments as support for Radical Reconstruction policies decreased.

CHAPTER PREVIEW

Comparison Study Foldable Make this foldable to help you compare and contrast Reconstruction in the Northern and Southern states.

Step 1 Mark the midpoint of the side edge of a sheet of paper.

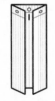

Draw a mark at the midpoint.

Step 2 Turn the paper and fold the edges in to touch at the midpoint.

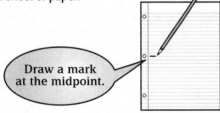

Step 3 Turn and label your foldable as shown.

Reading and Writing As you read the chapter, write facts that show how Reconstruction differed and was the same in the Northern states and Southern states. Write the facts in the appropriate places inside your foldable.

CHAPTER REVIEW

Foldables Follow-Up Activity

Have students use their completed foldables to write out a list of 10 similarities and differences concerning Reconstruction in the North and the South. Ask them to leave out a key term or phrase, and then trade their list with another classmate to complete. Have them return the lists to the authors for grading.

TEACHER NOTES

_____
_____
_____
_____
_____
_____
_____
_____
_____
_____
_____
_____
_____
_____
_____
_____

Alternative Activities for Chapter 17

EVALUATING

Using the same foldable design, have students explore Abraham Lincoln's plan for Reconstruction known as the Ten Percent Plan, and the plan passed by Congress, the Wade-Davis Bill. Students should write information regarding each plan under the appropriate tabs on their foldables. Have students write a paragraph comparing and contrasting the two plans for Reconstruction, and then ask students which they feel was the better plan.

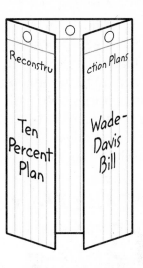

COMPARING

Have students compare and contrast the Fourteenth and Fifteenth Amendments. Suggest that students draw a Venn diagram on the inside of their foldables, listing the individual elements of each amendment under the appropriate tab, with the common elements of each amendment listed in the middle of the diagram. Ask students to consider the amendments' positive aspects, as well as how they fell short of ensuring equality for all American citizens.

Student Study Tip

Encourage students to spend some time becoming familiar with using library resources. Students should explore these various types of reference books: encyclopedias, biographical dictionaries, atlases, and almanacs. Students may use card catalogs, periodical guides, and/or computer databases to help them find the information they need.

Chapter 17 FOLDABLES

Reshaping the Nation

CHAPTER SUMMARY

Following the Civil War, settlers began to move west due to mineral discoveries. This led to conflict with Native Americans because settlers slaughtered buffalo, which Native American groups depended on for daily living. Immigrants came to the United States to settle in cities and work in factories but faced discrimination and poor living conditions. Progressive reform affected many areas of life and the United States took a more active role in international affairs to expand trade and power. The United States entered World War I in 1917 and helped the Allies win.

CHAPTER PREVIEW

Organizing Information Study Foldable

The content of Chapter 18 covers a large time span and many important events in American history. To help you understand a large amount of information, you must first organize it. Make this foldable to help you.

Step 1 Mark the midpoint of a side edge of one sheet of paper. Then fold the outside edges in to touch at the midpoint.

Step 2 Fold in half from side to side.

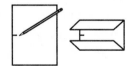

Step 3 Open and cut along the inside fold lines to form four tabs. Label your foldable as shown.

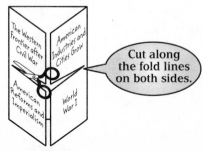

> Cut along the fold lines on both sides.

Reading and Writing As you read the chapter, write down key ideas under each appropriate tab.

CHAPTER REVIEW

Foldables Follow-Up Activity

Organize the class into small groups. Have students share their completed foldables with others in their groups in the following way. Students should take turns slowly reading their key ideas out loud. The other students should correctly identify the main subject category from the key ideas given.

TEACHER NOTES

_____
_____
_____
_____
_____
_____
_____
_____
_____
_____
_____
_____
_____
_____

Alternative Activities for Chapter 18

DRAWING CONCLUSIONS

Have students write four different groups on their foldables. Then have them write several difficulties that these groups faced under each appropriate tab using information from the chapter. As a class, discuss why students think these difficulties arose, and what groups they think have difficulties today.

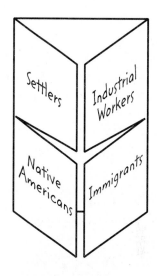

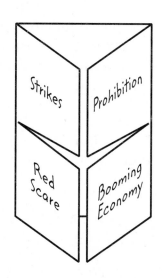

CAUSE AND EFFECT

Ask students to find four changes in the chapter that occurred in the 1920s and write them on their foldables. Inside, have them write out the causes and effects of each change. Organize the class into pairs and ask them to share their foldables with each other.

Student Study Tip

As students are learning the chapter, remind them that time lines are effective study guides, especially when a chapter spans 50 or more years. The time lines should include important events with a brief description about each event. This will enhance learning as students see how things happened chronologically.

Chapter 18 **FOLDABLES**

The Making of Modern America

CHAPTER SUMMARY

The United States entered World War II in 1941, leading the Allies to victory. As World War II ended, a bitter rivalry developed between the United States and the Soviet Union called the Cold War. Americans struggled with communism abroad and civil rights at home. Presidential scandals tested the American political system, but checks and balances prevented the abuse of power. The United States called for a worldwide coalition to fight against terrorism after suffering the worst terrorist attack in its history in September, 2001.

CHAPTER PREVIEW

Cause-Effect Information Study Foldable

Make this foldable to help you organize events and facts about the history of modern America from 1929 to the present.

Step 1 Fold one sheet of paper in half from side to side.

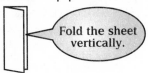

Fold the sheet vertically.

Step 2 Fold it again, 1 inch from the top. (**Tip:** The middle knuckle of your index finger is about 1 inch long.)

Step 3 Open and label as shown.

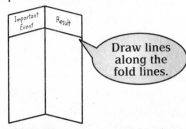

Important Event | Result

Draw lines along the fold lines.

Reading and Writing As you read this chapter, write down important events in the first column of your foldable. Then, in the second column, list some major results of each event listed in the first column.

CHAPTER REVIEW

Foldables Follow-Up Activity

Have students use their foldables to make a mini book of events. Alongside each important event from the chapter, ask them to draw the first thing that comes to mind or write one key word. By using associations, students can quickly remember things at a later date. Suggest they use colorful pens, and brainstorm with other classmates if they get stuck.

TEACHER NOTES

_____
_____
_____
_____
_____
_____
_____
_____
_____
_____
_____
_____
_____

Alternative Activities for Chapter 19

EXPLAINING

Have students write *Before: Road to War* in the first column of their foldables and *After: Effects of War* in the second column. Then have them list important events from the chapter that led to World War II under the first heading and how the nation was affected by the war under the second heading. Encourage students to discuss their foldables in small groups.

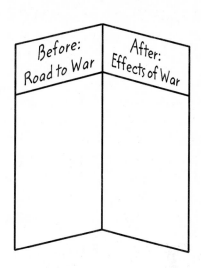

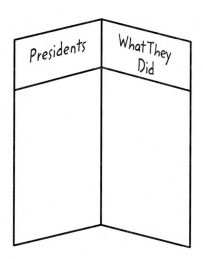

IDENTIFYING

Since Chapter 19 spans a number of years, students will benefit by listing all the presidents from the chapter on their foldables, and then writing what each president did during his presidency. Encourage them to list them consecutively so they can relate the presidents to the proper era. If you have time, have students create a matching quiz from their foldables to exchange with one another.

Student Study Tip

Taking good notes is important for successful learning. Share the five "R's" of note taking with your students. **Recording** involves writing down the main ideas. **Reducing** is summarizing. **Reciting** is reviewing lecture notes. **Reflecting** means thinking about what it is you are supposed to learn. Finally, **Reviewing** is essential to enforce the material. Place these on a bulletin board for students to read throughout the course.

Chapter 19 FOLDABLES